VINTAGE
QUILT REVIVAL

22 MODERN DESIGNS *from* CLASSIC BLO

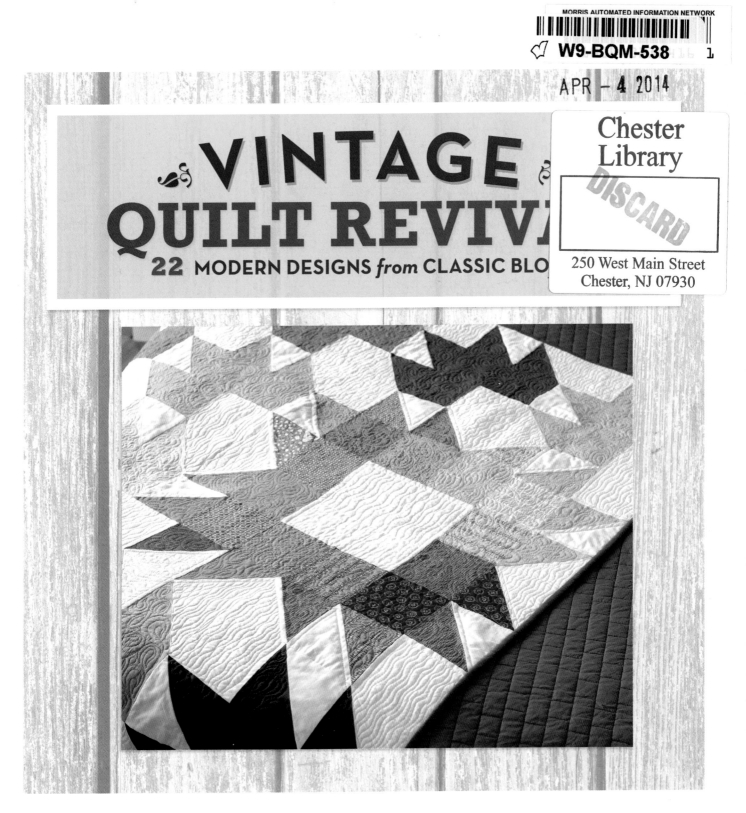

KATIE CLARK BLAKESLEY · LEE HEINRICH · FAITH JONES

INTERWEAVE.
interweave.com

ACKNOWLEDGMENTS

From Katie

This book is for my mother, Annette, and my mother-in-law, Jane, who taught me how to sew. And for my grandmothers, recent and past, who have made and appreciated quilts for a very long time.

Special thanks to my husband, Jayme, and my children, Lucas and Norah. Without their Saturday adventures, love, support, and willingness to watch PBS kid's shows, make brownies, and give me pep talks, this book wouldn't have happened.

Thank you to my friends, near and far, who offered encouragement, went on bike rides, swam laps with me, watched my kids, and cheered me on.

Finally, a special thanks to my coauthors, Lee and Faith, for being even better friends and women than they are designers, artists, and quilters. That is saying something. I'm so glad we took this journey together.

From Lee

I have so many people to thank for their love and support during this process! Thank you to my husband, Bob, who picked up the slack at home without a single complaint and who encouraged me to pursue this in the first place. Thank you to my wonderful daughters, Elsa and Claire, for learning the meaning of this new word "deadline." They showed an understanding beyond their years of what that meant for our family. And a special thanks to my mom, who started me on this journey by giving me my first sewing machine and sewing lesson. This book would not have been possible without you.

Thanks also to my friends in the Milwaukee Modern Quilt Guild, especially Rebecca Bark, Amy Wall, Erin Pann, and Linda Sullivan. They were enthusiastic pattern testers who made invaluable suggestions and were a wonderful support group. And thank you to Julie Karasek at Patched Works in Elm Grove, Wisconsin, and to Anne Books at Material Matters in Thiensville, Wisconsin, for being so supportive of me and my growing business.

Finally, I have to thank my amazing coauthors, Katie and Faith. I never could have navigated the insanity of writing a book without the two of you. I'm privileged to have been able to work with both of you and to call you my friends.

From Faith

To my mom, for teaching me how to sew and quilt. To my husband and children, for your love and support over the last two years while I worked on this book. To my coauthors, Katie and Lee, for your talent, creativity, and encouragement. I'm so blessed to be able to call you my friends.

From Katie, Lee, and Faith

Thank you to our editor, Cynthia Bix, who took a disorganized mess of a concept written by three people in separate parts of the country and turned it into something cohesive, organized, and readable. Thank you also to Linda Griepentrog for her excellent and very thorough technical editing. Both Cynthia's and Linda's knowledge, hard work, and calming influence were invaluable. Finally, thank you to Michael Miller Fabrics (www .michaelmillerfabrics.com) and Aurifil Thread (www.aurifil.com) for providing some of the materials used in this book.

EDITOR
Cynthia Bix

TECHNICAL EDITOR
Linda Turner Griepentrog

ASSOCIATE ART DIRECTOR
Julia Boyles

COVER & INTERIOR DESIGNER
Adrian Newman

TECHNICAL ILLUSTRATOR
Missy Shepler

PHOTOGRAPHER
Joe Hancock

PRODUCTION
Katherine Jackson

Interweave
A division of F+W Media, Inc.
201 East Fourth Street
Loveland, CO 80537
interweave.com

Manufactured in China by RR Donnelley Shenzhen.

Library of Congress
Cataloging-in-Publication Data
Blakesley, Katie.
 Vintage quilt revival : 22 modern designs from classic blocks / Katie Blakesley, Lee Heinrich, and Faith Jones.
 pages cm
 Includes bibliographical references and index.
 ISBN 978-1-62033-054-8 (pbk)
 ISBN 978-1-62033-055-5 (PDF)
 1. Quilting--Patterns. I. Heinrich, Lee. II. Jones, Faith, 1977- III. Title.
 TT835.B5122 2013
 746.46'041--dc23
 2013018274

10 9 8 7 6 5 4 3 2 1

CONTENTS

INTRODUCTION

We three authors feel fortunate to have personal connections with the quilts of the past. As a child, Katie was surrounded by beautiful quilts that were handmade by her grandmother, great-grandmothers, and great-great-grandmothers. When she visited her grandmother's home, the beds always had special quilts on them. Lee spent her childhood sleeping under an antique quilt that had been made by her great-grandmother and the women of a rural Depression-era quilting bee. That quilt was on Lee's bed for years and still has a special place in her heart. Faith's childhood memories include many visits to local antiques shops, as her mother searched for and collected handmade quilts from past generations. These antique quilts were always stacked and draped in rooms throughout the house. None of the three of us gave much thought to becoming quilters until we were well into adulthood, but vintage quilts and the women who made them played a role in our lives from the beginning.

Our paths may be somewhat unique—not everyone is lucky enough to have a family heritage of quilting. But the end result for all of us is the same: We love the creative process that starts with a pile of beautiful fabric and ends in a unique handmade quilt. As the three of us continued to search for inspiration in new and different places, we were drawn to the quilts of our heritage—the quilts of the past.

In the summer of 2011, the three of us joined together to host on our blogs a series of online tutorials based on vintage quilt blocks. For the "Summer Sampler Series," we each chose four blocks from Barbara Brackman's *Encyclopedia of Pieced Quilt Patterns* and provided step-by-step instructions, foundation-piecing templates, technique tutorials, and even a bit of the history behind the blocks.

We love the creative process that starts with a pile of beautiful fabric . . . we were drawn to the quilts of our heritage—the quilts of the past.

We finished the series determined to learn more about traditional piecing and vintage quilts and were pleased to realize that a number of vintage quilts, especially many made in the nineteenth and early twentieth centuries, fit the current working definition of modern quilting. Modern quilting typically includes at least one of the following: improvisational piecing; asymmetrical design; simplicity instead of fussiness; on-trend color combinations (often including the use of solids); utilitarian use and design; and reference to nature, architecture, and modern art as sources of inspiration.

More and more frequently, quilters of all backgrounds have become interested in "traditional-to-modern" quilting, led by pioneers such as Denyse Schmidt. Quilters looking for a new muse and seeking to improve their techniques are starting to discover and recognize traditional patterns as a treasure trove of inspiration. Likewise, many quilters from a more traditional background are becoming interested in aspects of modern quilting and how to blend elements of each into a single project.

Vintage Quilt Revival invites readers to use vintage quilt blocks to create unique works of art. In our book, you will find step-by-step instructions for making twenty traditional quilt blocks, along with a complete project and three sampler quilts using each of these blocks, as well as mini history lessons and design tips for making traditional blocks fresh and modern for the twenty-first century. We also offer brief tutorials on the basics of some important techniques, including foundation piecing, to help you along your way.

Spin It Again Quilt, made by Lee Heinrich (page 86)

*Double Dutch Table Runner,
made by Katie Clark Blakesley (page 118)*

Unlike our original "Summer Sampler Series," our emphasis here is not on the sampler quilt itself—although we do include instructions for three unique sampler quilts using the blocks in this book. Instead, our focus is to provide you with fresh quilt layouts, simple and detailed instructions, and solid strategies for using vintage blocks in new and original ways.

We hope *Vintage Quilt Revival* inspires you to improve your sewing skills and to try a new technique. If you are a beginning quilter or are new to foundation piecing, just take things step by step. Cut a sample block and piece it together before cutting out all of your fabric, or you may have to re-cut (something that has happened to us more than once). Although there are some quicker small-scale projects and quilts in this book, we hope you will enjoy working on some of these quilts over weeks or even months, and that you will enjoy not only the end product, but the process as well. Remember—there is something inherently beautiful in the imperfection of a handmade item. Embrace the "skill-building moments" as they come.

We believe that learning the history of our craft and something of the quilters before us makes us better-informed and more innovative quilters. We hope you will be inspired to learn more about vintage quilts (and the quilters who made them) and will visit a local textile or folk art museum. Whether you decide to create a nontraditional block repeat, include more negative space in a quilt design, use multiple blocks to create unique secondary patterns, or vary the size of your blocks, our goal is to provide examples and tools that we hope will encourage you to make quilts that fit into the burgeoning "traditional-made-modern" movement.

Katie Clark Blakesley

[signature]

[signature]

HOW TO USE THIS BOOK

Vintage Quilt Revival is, first and foremost, a book about possibilities—the fresh possibilities inherent in the classic quilt blocks of the past. As you flip through this book and consider which projects to make, we hope you will think not only in terms of the individual blocks and patterns included here, but also of all the creative design possibilities these blocks provide. We've attempted to give you the tools you need to do just that.

For each block featured in this book, you will find four sections:

A BLOCK TUTORIAL, with instructions for making a single classic quilt block at 12" × 12" (30.5 × 30.5 cm) finished size. You can use these block tutorials to make the sampler quilts featured on pages 147–157. They also make great bee or swap blocks.

A PATTERN FOR A COMPLETE PROJECT using that block. These patterns include quilts, a table runner, a pillow, a bag, a zipper pouch, and more. The patterns do not always use the block at the same size as in the block tutorial, or the block may be pieced in a slightly different way. These differences are always noted in the pattern.

DESIGN NOTES—a discussion of the strategies we used to modernize the block in the project pattern. While the design tips included here are specific to the block or project, most of these strategies could be applied to all of the blocks in the book—or to any other traditional quilt block.

MINI HISTORY LESSONS—tidbits of information about the traditions of quilting and how the past is impacting quilters today.

One of the things that inspired us to write this book is the versatility of these classic blocks when used in today's quilts. Our goal was to set up the book in a way that would encourage

Sampler Quilt in Solids,
made by Katie Clark Blakesley (page 150)

you to embrace this versatility. You'll see that the projects using the blocks are presented in three different sections—New Settings, New Color Approaches, and Re-Imagined Blocks—according to the way in which we've updated the block or the pattern.

Try swapping the blocks used in the patterns or apply one of the design strategies we suggest in our Design Notes to a completely different project of your own. We hope you'll agree that the possibilities are endless.

20 CLASSIC BLOCKS

Sampler Quilt, On-Point, made by Faith Jones (page 154)

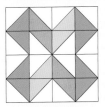

Double Z
(Geometric Slide Quilt,
page 18)

Dakota Star
(Stardust Quilt, page 24)

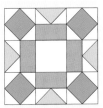

Riviera
(Stardust Quilt, page 24)

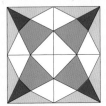

Rolling Squares
(Dancing Squares Quilt,
page 30)

Red Cross
(Cross Point Quilt,
page 38)

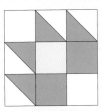

Mayflower
(New World Pouch,
page 44)

Tea Leaf
(Spiced Chai Quilt,
page 50)

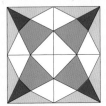

Crosspatch
(Crosspatch Bag,
page 56)

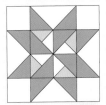

Star-and-Pinwheel
(Sugar Snow Quilt,
page 62)

Mosaic No. 19
(Sorbet Mini Quilt,
page 74)

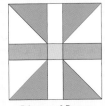

Diamond Panes
(Rosy Windows Quilt,
page 80)

Wheel of Fortune
(Spin It Again Quilt,
page 86)

Tilted Star
(Cosmos Baby Quilt,
page 92)

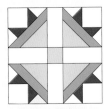

Cross and Crown
(Seaside Quilt, page 98)

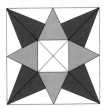

Exploding Star
(Star Bright Quilt,
page 104)

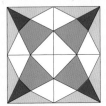

Geometric Star
(Cut Glass Baby Quilt,
page 112)

Double Windmill
(Double Dutch Table
Runner, page 118)

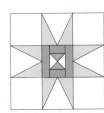

Dove at the Window,
(Twinkle Mini Quilt
page 126)

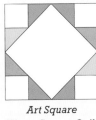

Art Square
(Times Square Quilt,
page 134)

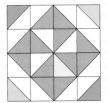

Mosaic No. 8
(Rainbow Mosaic Pillow,
page 140)

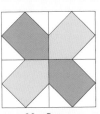

Introduction: 20 CLASSIC BLOCKS **9**

TOOLS AND TECHNIQUES

Before you begin, we offer a quick review of some basic tools you'll need to make the projects in this book.

As for quiltmaking techniques, this book assumes that you have a good working knowledge of basic quilting skills. Some projects do call for specific piecing techniques:

• Foundation piecing and/or

• Partial seams.

We've included brief tutorials on these techniques that can serve to refresh your memory or, if you're a beginner, to get you started on your way to making innovative quilts.

TOOLS AND MATERIALS CHECKLIST

To make beautiful quilts, start with the right tools. We've put together a list of some of the tools and materials that any quilter—from beginner to expert—will need. There may be many other items that could be added to this collection, depending on individual preferences, but we hope this list will serve as a good starting point for building your own quilter's toolbox.

- ❑ Sewing machine

- ❑ Optional sewing machine feet such as a quarter-inch piecing foot, an open-toe foot for foundation piecing, a walking foot, and a free-motion quilting foot or darning foot

- ❑ Sewing machine needles for piecing, foundation piecing, and quilting (Foundation piecing requires more frequent needle changes than other types of piecing, since the paper quickly dulls the needles.)

- ❑ Handsewing needles for quilt binding

- ❑ Rotary cutter

- ❑ Clear acrylic rotary cutting rulers in a variety of sizes (A 6" × 24" (15 × 61 cm) and 12½" (30.5 cm) square are particularly handy for the projects in this book.)

- ❑ Self-healing cutting mat

- ❑ Iron and ironing board

- ❑ Seam ripper

- ❑ Scissors

- ❑ Optional glue stick or double-sided tape for adhering fabric pieces to the foundation-piecing patterns

- ❑ Straight pins

- ❑ Curved safety pins for basting or basting spray

- ❑ Pincushion or magnetic pin holder

- ❑ Pencil

- ❑ Chopstick or point turner

- ❑ Fabric marker (water-soluble or air-soluble pen; tailor's chalk; or a Hera marker, which makes a crease instead of a mark)

- ❑ Masking tape for taping quilt tops down while basting

- ❑ Paper for foundation piecing (We use standard photocopy paper.)

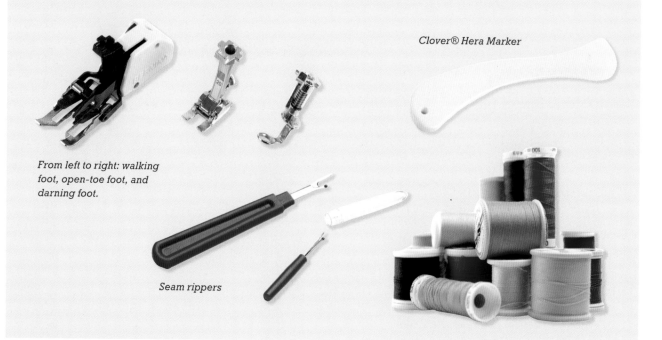

Clover® Hera Marker

From left to right: walking foot, open-toe foot, and darning foot.

Seam rippers

TECHNIQUES

Accurate piecing is important for ensuring that your quilts come together successfully. Of course, practice makes (almost) perfect, but there are other things you can do to improve the accuracy of your piecing. Cutting fabrics carefully and sewing with a perfect ¼" (6 mm) or even a *scant* ¼" (6 mm) seam allowance will help. Foundation piecing greatly improves accuracy, as does careful trimming. Following are brief, basic tutorials for foundation piecing and sewing partial seams.

Guide to foundation piecing

Foundation piecing, also called paper piecing, is the process of sewing fabric together onto a foundation such as a paper template. This technique allows for extremely accurate piecing of the most complex designs. On each foundation-piecing template are numbered pieces, or sections. Always start with number one and work through them in sequence until you reach the end of the numbered pieces.

Note: *In the diagrams, the shaded areas represent the wrong side of the fabric.*

1 The template patterns for the projects can be found on a CD included with this book. Print the required number of templates specified for your quilt project at 100 percent. When printing, be sure to uncheck the box that says "fit to page" or "scale" so the images print at their actual size.

2 Cut out the templates. Make sure to include the extra ¼" (6 mm) border around each template for the seam allowance.

3 Cut out the fabric pieces as specified in the quilt project.

4 Reduce your sewing machine stitch length. We typically use 1.4 mm or about eighteen stitches per inch (stitch length setting indicators vary on different machine brands). You will be stitching through both fabric and paper, and the needle will perforate the paper. This reduced stitch length allows the paper to tear off easily when it's time to remove it.

5 Begin with the cut fabric for template piece 1. With the printed side of the paper template facing up, place the fabric right side out on the back (unprinted side) of the paper template *(fig. 1)*. Cover the entire area of template piece 1 with fabric, plus ¼" (6 mm) hanging over any seam lines. Pin in place.

Sampler Quilt in Solids, made by Katie Clark Blakesley (page 150)

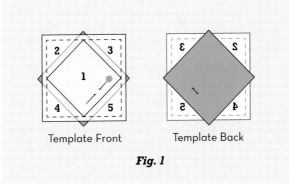

Template Front   Template Back

Fig. 1

6 Take the cut fabric for template piece 2. Place it on the back of the paper template, right sides together with piece 1, pinned into place in the previous step. Hold the template up to the light and make sure at least ¼" (6 mm) of the fabric overlaps into adjacent template spaces for the seam allowance *(fig. 2)*.

7 With the paper template printed side faceup and the pinned fabric side facedown, stitch along the printed seam line between pieces 1 and 2. Make sure to stitch ¼" (6 mm) beyond the beginning and ending of the printed seam line, as this is the seam allowance for the intersecting piece(s). Open out piece 2 and press the seam *(fig. 3)*.

8 Repeat this process until the entire paper template is pieced in number sequence *(fig. 4)*.

9 faceup. Using a quilting ruler and rotary cutter, trim around the block leaving a ¼" (6 mm) seam allowance around the entire template *(fig. 5)*.

10 Carefully tear away the paper. Use tweezers or a straight pin to remove smaller pieces of paper.

Guide to partial seams

Sewing a partial seam is the process of sewing a seam part of the way, then returning at a later time to finish sewing the rest of seam.

Note: In the diagrams, the shaded areas represent the wrong side of the fabric.

1 When sewing partial seams, it's helpful to lay out the fabric pieces first to visualize the sewing order *(fig. 6)*. In this example, the block is similar to a traditional Log Cabin block.

2 Place the center square and one fabric edge right sides together matching the left edges and stitch a ¼" (6 mm) seam about half the length of the center square *(fig. 7)*. Backstitch and then press the seam as desired. Leave the second half of the fabric unsewn until the last step.

3 Working around the center, piece the edge fabrics to the center block sequentially as you would normally piece a Log Cabin block *(fig. 8)*.

Note: If you have not pieced a traditional Log Cabin block, refer to a basic quiltmaking book or Web tutorial.

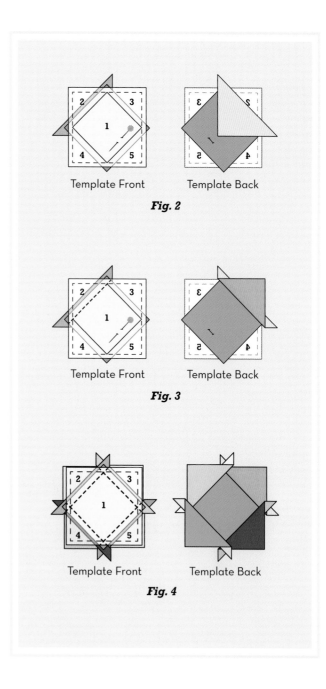

Template Front   Template Back
Fig. 2

Template Front   Template Back
Fig. 3

Template Front   Template Back
Fig. 4

4 After all sides are pieced, return to the partially sewn seam from Step 2. Finish stitching the original seam length *(fig. 9)*, backstitching at the beginning of seam.

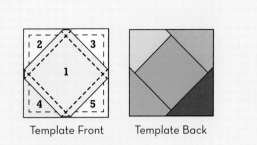

Template Front   Template Back

Fig. 5

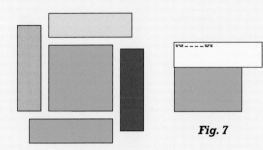

Fig. 6

Fig. 7

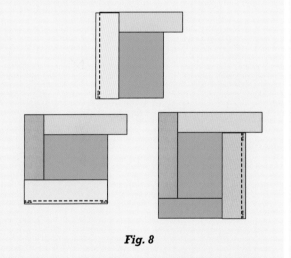

Fig. 8

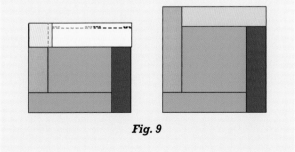

Fig. 9

A few general piecing hints

Follow these simple "rules" as you piece your projects.

Pin or baste before stitching to hold things in place.

All seams are ¼" (6 mm) unless otherwise noted, and sewn right sides together.

Align and nest all adjacent seams.

Press seams toward the darker fabric, unless otherwise noted.

You may notice that, in some cases, projects in this book present different ways of accomplishing the same block or block elements. This is particularly true of methods for making Flying Geese and half-square triangles. You are free to use whatever method you prefer; just be sure to adjust the amounts of fabric you buy and cut accordingly.

Stardust Quilt, made by Lee Heinrich (page 24)

❧ NEW SETTINGS ❧

In this section, we feature traditional blocks in a variety of new, fresh settings. We provide tips and tricks for changing up the ever-popular grid pattern, such as four blocks across by five blocks down with 3" (7.5 mm) of sashing between each block. Whether it's incorporating negative space, staggering the blocks in rows, using the same block in a variety of sizes, combining different blocks to create secondary patterns, turning blocks on end, or a combination of these methods, we hope you come away with a fresh perspective on block settings that you can apply to any of your favorite blocks and patterns.

BLOCK:
Double Z

PROJECT:
Geometric Slide Quilt

*Designed and made by **Faith Jones***

FINISHED SIZE:	TECHNIQUE USED:	SKILL LEVEL:
60" × 60" (152.5 × 152.5 cm)	Simple piecing	Beginner

DESIGN NOTE: | *Staggering Quilt Blocks*

The modern quilt movement encourages us to think about alternatives to traditional quilt top layouts. One principle the Modern Quilt Guild cites in this new style of quilting is simplicity. (For more about the Guild, see page 54.) Creating a striking quilt does not always mean covering the entire quilt top with patchwork. When designing the Geometric Slide Quilt, I arranged the blocks in a simple staggered layout, which creates a feeling of motion around the quilt. The remaining columns of negative space give the eye a place to rest when taking in this sharp, geometric design.

Some quilters may be worried about the amount of white in a minimalist design such as this quilt. Maybe the recipient is a child, and the quilt is sure to be well loved (dragged around on the floor, spilled on, and slept with every night). If you are concerned about the light background color, consider replacing the background with a single print, and use your solid neutral, such as tan or white, as the piecing in the block. The bold design choice of inverting the original pattern will lead to dramatic results.

CLASSIC DOUBLE Z BLOCK

UNFINISHED BLOCK: 12½" × 12½" (31.5 × 31.5 cm)

Choose scraps from your stash to make this classic version for a block swap or bee. If you want to make it for a sampler quilt, see pages 146–157. To make the Geometric Slide Quilt version, see opposite page.

Cutting

FROM WHITE FABRIC, CUT:

☐ 8 squares 4¼" × 4¼" (11 × 11 cm); cut in half diagonally to make 16 half-square triangles.

FROM GREEN FABRIC, CUT:

☐ 2 squares 4¼" × 4¼" (11 × 11 cm); cut in half diagonally to make 4 half-square triangles.

FROM ORANGE FABRIC, CUT:

☐ 2 squares 4¼" × 4¼" (11 × 11 cm); cut in half diagonally to make 4 half-square triangles.

FROM YELLOW FABRIC, CUT:

☐ 2 squares 4¼" × 4¼" (11 × 11 cm); cut in half diagonally to make 4 half-square triangles.

FROM AQUA FABRIC, CUT:

☐ 2 squares 4¼" × 4¼" (11 × 11 cm); cut in half diagonally to make 4 half-square triangles.

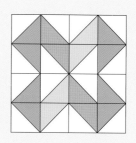

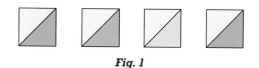

Fig. 1

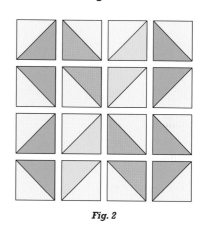

Fig. 2

Assembling the Block

1. Pair *each* white half-square triangle with a colored half-square triangle, right sides together. Sew along the diagonal edge to create sixteen squares *(fig. 1)*.

2. Align a 45-degree ruler line with the seam and trim the squares to 3½" × 3½" (9 × 9 cm). Lay them out as shown *(fig. 2)*.

3. Sew the squares together into four rows of four squares each. Sew the rows together to make the block. Press.

MAKE THE GEOMETRIC SLIDE QUILT

Materials

All fabric amounts are for 45" (114.5 cm) wide fabric.

- 3 yd (2.75 m) white fabric
- ½ yd (45.5 cm) red fabric
- ½ yd (45.5 cm) orange fabric
- ½ yd (45.5 cm) yellow fabric
- ½ yd (45.5 cm) blue fabric
- 3⅞ yd (3.6 m) backing fabric
- 68" × 68" (172.7 × 172.7 cm) low-loft cotton batting
- ⅝ yd (57 cm) binding fabric

Cutting

FROM WHITE FABRIC, CUT:

❒ 80 squares 4¼" × 4¼" (11 cm × 11 cm); cut in half diagonally to make 160 half-square triangles.

❒ 2 rectangles 6½" × 12½" (16.5 × 31.5 cm).

❒ 2 squares 12½" × 12½" (31.5 × 31.5 cm).

❒ 2 rectangles 12½" × 18½" (31.5 × 47 cm).

❒ 2 rectangles 12½" × 24½" (31.5 × 62 cm).

❒ 2 strips 12½" × 30½" (31.5 × 77.5 cm).

FROM RED FABRIC, CUT:

❒ 20 squares 4¼" × 4¼" (11 × 11 cm); cut in half diagonally to make 40 half-square triangles.

FROM ORANGE FABRIC, CUT:

❒ 20 squares 4¼" × 4¼" (11 × 11 cm); cut in half diagonally to make 40 half-square triangles.

FROM YELLOW FABRIC, CUT:

❒ 20 squares 4¼" × 4¼" (11 × 11 cm); cut in half diagonally to create 40 half-square triangles.

FROM BLUE FABRIC, CUT:

❒ 20 squares 4¼" × 4¼" (11 × 11 cm); cut in half diagonally to make 40 half-square triangles.

FROM BINDING FABRIC, CUT:

❒ 7 strips 2½" (6.5 cm) × width of fabric.

Double Z Blocks

UNFINISHED BLOCK:

12½" × 12½" (31.5 × 31.5 cm)

Follow the Classic Double Z Block instructions to make ten blocks. Refer to the block illustration for color placement.

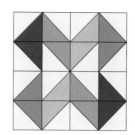

Quilt Top

1 Lay out the ten blocks and the ten white pieces (two squares and eight rectangles) in five columns as shown in the Geometric Slide Construction Diagram.

2 Sew together the pieces in each column and press. Sew together the columns to create a finished quilt top. Press the seams open to reduce bulk.

3 Make a quilt sandwich with the backing, batting, and quilt top. Baste the layers and quilt as desired. I used an allover stippling on the project quilt. Trim the batting and backing to match the quilt top.

4 Join the binding strips to make a continuous length. Bind the raw edges to finish the quilt.

MINI HISTORY LESSON: *Amish Quilts*

The Amish community is known for quilts that feature geometric shapes and negative space. The designs have a spare quality, relying on large geometric fields of color instead of on patchwork. For these reasons, they often look "modern" to our eyes.

Early Amish quilts were typically made using just a few dark-colored solid fabrics. In Geometric Slide, this feature has been reversed and makes use of a plain white background instead of a dark one.

Amish quilts were handquilted, usually by groups of women. The quilting was often intricate, in contrast to the simple quilt design. As time passed, additional colors and simple patterns such as the Nine Patch were incorporated into the quilts. Later, basket and floral designs appeared. Today, some of the Amish community partners with well-known fabric and quilt designers, such as Denyse Schmidt's Couture Quilt line, to create quilts for sale.

Geometric Slide Construction Diagram

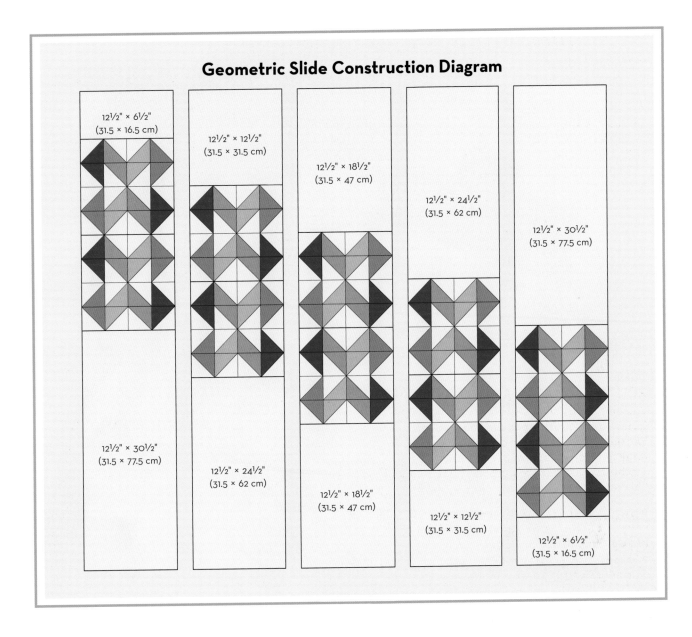

12 1/2" × 6 1/2"
(31.5 × 16.5 cm)

12 1/2" × 12 1/2"
(31.5 × 31.5 cm)

12 1/2" × 18 1/2"
(31.5 × 47 cm)

12 1/2" × 24 1/2"
(31.5 × 62 cm)

12 1/2" × 30 1/2"
(31.5 × 77.5 cm)

12 1/2" × 30 1/2"
(31.5 × 77.5 cm)

12 1/2" × 24 1/2"
(31.5 × 62 cm)

12 1/2" × 18 1/2"
(31.5 × 47 cm)

12 1/2" × 12 1/2"
(31.5 × 31.5 cm)

12 1/2" × 6 1/2"
(31.5 × 16.5 cm)

BLOCKS:
Riviera and Dakota Star

PROJECT:
Stardust Quilt

Designed and made by **Lee Heinrich**

FINISHED SIZE:	TECHNIQUE USED:	SKILL LEVEL:
60" × 72" (152.5 × 182.9 cm)	Foundation piecing	Intermediate

DESIGN NOTE: | *Using secondary patterns*

One of the most interesting design elements in a quilt—and one that often is overlooked—is the "secondary pattern" created by repeating blocks. The secondary pattern is the design that materializes between repeated blocks, so it may not be obvious until four or more blocks are placed together.

To create a dazzling secondary pattern, try combining two different blocks. To combine blocks effectively, look for designs that will create unbroken lines extending from one block into the other. In the case of the Stardust Quilt, the Dakota Star angled seams continue right into the Riviera block seams, extending and enlarging the star shape in the Riviera block.

Once you're happy with your secondary design, use value to play it up and make it "pop." Darker values recede, while lighter values come forward, so I chose to use mostly lighter values within the secondary star shape in the Stardust Quilt. Darker values outside of that shape help further define it for the viewer.

CLASSIC RIVIERA BLOCK

UNFINISHED BLOCK: 12½" × 12½" (31.5 × 31.5 cm)

Choose scraps from your stash to make this classic version for a block swap or bee. If you want to make it for a sampler quilt, see pages 146–157. To make the Stardust Quilt version, see page 28. Riviera templates A and B are on the CD included with this book.

Cutting

FROM WHITE FABRIC, CUT:

- ❑ 4 rectangles 3½" × 4" (9 × 10 cm) (template piece A1).

- ❑ 4 strips 2½" × 6" (6.5 × 15 cm) (template piece A3).

- ❑ 4 strips 3" × 7" (7.5 × 18 cm) (template piece B1).

- ❑ 4 rectangles 2½" × 5" (6.5 × 12.5 cm) (template piece B3).

FROM YELLOW FABRIC, CUT:

- ❑ 4 rectangles 2½" × 5" (6.5 × 12.5 cm) (template piece A2).

FROM RED FABRIC, CUT:

- ❑ 4 strips 3½" × 7" (9 × 18 cm) (template piece A4).

FROM ORANGE FABRIC, CUT:

- ❑ 4 strips 2½" × 6" (6.5 × 15 cm) (template piece B2).

FROM GREEN FABRIC, CUT:

- ❑ 4 rectangles 3½" × 4" (9 × 10 cm) (template piece B4).

Assembling the Block

1. Print and cut out four *each* of Riviera block templates A and B.

2. Using the technique described in Guide to Foundation Piecing (page 13), piece eight templates. Use the cutting instructions to identify which fabric pieces correspond to each template number.

3. Sew each Section A to a Section B piece along the diagonal edges *(fig. 1)*.

4. Sew together the four units into a completed Riviera block *(fig. 2)*.

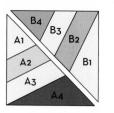

Fig. 1

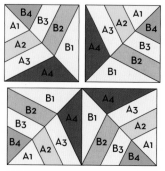

Fig. 2

> **Tip**
> *Template A and B numbers are reversed. This means that the seams will be pressed in opposite directions, allowing for easier seam alignment when the sections are joined.*

CLASSIC DAKOTA STAR BLOCK

UNFINISHED BLOCK: 12½" × 12½" (31.5 × 31.5 cm)

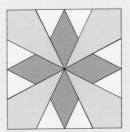

Choose scraps from your stash to make this classic version for a block swap or bee. If you want to make it for a sampler quilt, see pages 146–157. To make the Stardust Quilt version, see page 28. The Dakota Star foundation-piecing and cutting templates are on the CD included with this book.

Cutting

FROM GREEN FABRIC, CUT:

☐ 4 rectangles 4" × 7" (10 × 18 cm) (template piece 1).

FROM WHITE FABRIC, CUT:

☐ 8 rectangles 3¾" × 4¾" (9.5 × 12 cm) (template pieces 2 and 3).

FROM YELLOW FABRIC, CUT:

☐ Use the Dakota Star Cutting Template to cut 4.

Assembling the Block

1. Print and cut out four copies of the Dakota Star Foundation-piecing Template and one copy of the Dakota Star Cutting Template at 100 percent.

2. Using the technique described in Guide to Foundation Piecing (page 13), piece each of the Dakota Star Foundation-piecing Templates. Use the cutting instructions above to identify which fabric pieces correspond to each template number.

3. Sew each foundation-pieced section to one of the yellow pieces, right sides together *(fig. 1)*.

4. Sew together the four units into a completed Dakota Star block *(fig. 2)*.

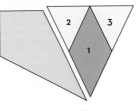

Fig. 1

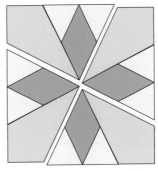

Fig. 2

MAKE THE STARDUST QUILT

Materials

All fabric amounts are for 45" (114.5 cm) wide fabric.

• 4 yd (3.7 m) white solid fabric

• 1¾ yd (1.6 m) light blue solid fabric

• 2½ yd (2.3 m) lime green solid fabric

• 1 yd (91.5 cm) gold solid fabric

• ¾ yd (68.5 cm) chartreuse solid fabric

• ¾ yd (68. 5 cm) aqua solid fabric

• ¾ yd (68.5 cm) bright yellow solid fabric

• 3⅔ yd (3.4 m) backing fabric

• 68" × 80" (172.7 × 203.2 cm) low-loft cotton batting

• ⅝ yd (57 cm) binding fabric

Tools

• Riviera Templates A and B, and Dakota Star Foundation-piecing and Cutting Templates*

• Foundation-piecing paper

• Piece of cardboard or template plastic *(optional)*

*You will need to print sixty copies of **each** Riviera and Dakota Star template at 100 percent. To make this many pieces, trace the cutting templates onto cardboard or template plastic for more durability.*

Cutting

FROM WHITE SOLID FABRIC CUT:

❏ 60 rectangles 3½" × 4" (9 × 10 cm) (Riviera Template piece B4).

❏ 60 strips 2½" × 6" (6.5 × 15 cm) (Rivier Template piece B2).

❏ 60 strips 3½" × 7" (9 × 18 cm) (Riviera Template piece A4).

❏ 60 rectangles 2½" × 5" (6.5 × 12.5 cm) (Riviera Template piece A2).

❏ 60 rectangles 4" × 7" (10 × 18 cm) (Dakota Star Foundation-piecing Template piece 1).

FROM LIGHT BLUE SOLID FABRIC, CUT:

❏ 120 rectangles 3¾" × 4¾" (9.5 × 12 cm) (Dakota Star Foundation-piecing Template pieces 2 and 3).

FROM LIME GREEN SOLID FABRIC, CUT:

❏ 60 pieces (Dakota Star Cutting Template).

FROM GOLD SOLID FABRIC, CUT:

❏ 60 rectangles 3½" × 7" (9 × 18 cm) (Riviera Template piece B1).

FROM CHARTREUSE SOLID FABRIC, CUT:

❏ 60 rectangles 3½" × 4" (9 × 10 cm) (Riviera Template piece A1).

FROM AQUA SOLID FABRIC, CUT:

❏ 60 rectangles 2½" × 5" (6.5 × 12.5 cm) (Riviera Template piece B3).

FROM BRIGHT YELLOW SOLID, CUT:

❏ 60 strips 2½" × 6" (6.5 × 15 cm) (Riviera Template piece A3).

FROM BINDING FABRIC, CUT:

❏ 7 strips 2½" (6.5 cm) × width of fabric.

Riviera and Dakota Star Blocks

UNFINISHED BLOCKS:

12½" × 12½" (31.5 × 31.5 cm)

Use the cutting instructions to identify which fabric pieces correspond to each template number.

1 Follow the Classic Riviera block instructions (page 26) to make fifteen Riviera blocks.

2 Follow the Classic Dakota Star block instructions (page 27) to make fifteen Dakota Star blocks.

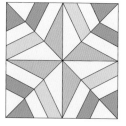

Riviera

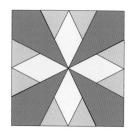

Dakota Star

Quilt Top

1 Lay out the blocks as shown in the Stardust Construction Diagram, alternating Riviera blocks and Dakota Star blocks.

2 Sew the blocks together in six rows of five blocks each, taking care to align the seams between the blocks. Press the seams toward the Riviera blocks.

3 Sew together the rows to create a finished quilt top. Press the seams open to reduce bulk.

4 Make a quilt sandwich with the backing, batting, and quilt top. Baste the layers and quilt as desired. I chose to do outline stitching on the stars, with stippling on the green background, so the stars really "pop." Trim the batting and backing to match the quilt top.

5 Join the binding strips to make a continuous length. Bind the raw edges to finish the quilt.

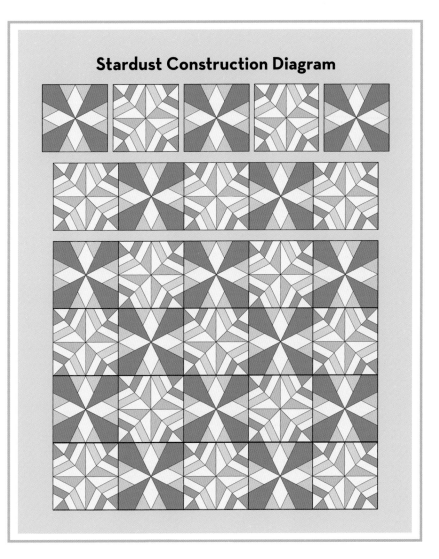

Stardust Construction Diagram

BLOCK:
Rolling Squares

PROJECT:
Dancing Squares Quilt

Designed and made by **Lee Heinrich**

FINISHED SIZE:	TECHNIQUE USED:	SKILL LEVEL:
51" × 68" (129.5 × 172.7 cm)	Foundation piecing	Intermediate

DESIGN NOTE:	*Using Negative Space*

"Negative space" in quilting refers to an area in a quilt design that is intentionally left blank or unpieced. It's often thought of as an iconic feature of modern quilts, but using negative space doesn't have to mean a minimalist composition with vast expanses of white.

Looking at the Dancing Squares quilt, you would hardly know at first glance that this quilt is made up entirely of Rolling Squares blocks, because I've used negative space to change the way the blocks interact with each other. The blocks are set on point, and color is strategically dropped out or added from the pieced sections to achieve this design. This is something that could easily be done with most (maybe even all) of the blocks in this book—or with any other traditional block. Play around with negative space to see what unique design variations you can create.

CLASSIC ROLLING SQUARES BLOCK

UNFINISHED BLOCK: 12½" × 12½" (31.5 × 31.5 cm)

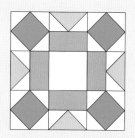

This block combines foundation-pieced units with Flying Geese units. Alternatively, the Flying Geese units can also be foundation pieced using the optional template. Choose scraps from your stash to make this classic version for a block swap or bee. If you want to make it for a sampler quilt, see pages 146–157. To make the Dancing Squares Quilt version, see page 34. The Rolling Squares Template and optional Flying Geese Template are on the CD included with this book.

Cutting

FROM WHITE FABRIC, CUT:

❏ 8 squares 3½" × 3½" (9 × 9 cm); cut in half diagonally to make 16 half-square triangles (Rolling Squares template pieces 2, 3, 4, and 5).

❏ 1 square 4½" × 4½" (11.5 × 11.5 cm).

❏ 4 squares 2⅞" × 2⅞" (7.3 × 7.3 cm); cut in half diagonally to make 8 half-square triangles (Flying Geese).

FROM AQUA FABRIC, CUT:

❏ 4 squares 3½" × 3½" (9 × 9 cm) (Rolling Squares template piece 1).

FROM YELLOW FABRIC, CUT:

❏ 1 square 5¼" × 5¼" (13.5 × 13.5 cm) (Flying Geese).

FROM ORANGE FABRIC, CUT:

❏ 4 rectangles 2½" × 4½" (6.5 × 11.5 cm).

Assembling the Block

1. Print and cut out four copies of the Rolling Squares Template at 100 percent. (A template is provided if you want to use it to make the Flying Geese; if so, print four.)

2. Using the technique described in Guide to Foundation Piecing (page 13), piece four Rolling Squares Templates. Use the cutting instructions to identify which fabric pieces correspond to each template number.

3. To create Flying Geese units, cut the yellow square 5¼" × 5¼" (13.5 × 13.5 cm) in half diagonally twice to create four quarter-square triangles *(fig. 1)*.

4. Sew a white 2⅞" (7.3 cm) half-square triangle to one edge of a yellow triangle, right sides together. Make sure the bottom edges of the white half-square triangle and the yellow triangle are aligned *(fig. 2)*.

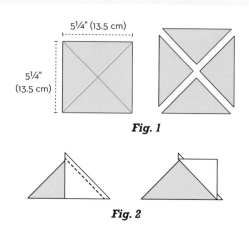

Fig. 1

Fig. 2

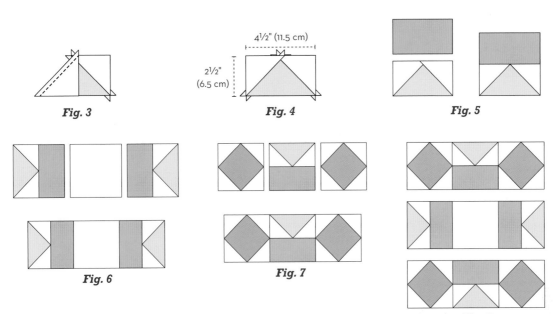

Fig. 3

4½" (11.5 cm)

2½" (6.5 cm)

Fig. 4

Fig. 5

Fig. 6

Fig. 7

Fig. 8

5. Repeat Step 4 with another white half-square triangle on the other edge of the yellow triangle to complete the Flying Geese unit *(fig. 3)*. Press seams open. The unit should now measure 2½" × 4½" (6.5 × 11.5 cm) *(fig. 4)*. Make four.

6. Match up each Flying Geese unit with an orange rectangle 2½" × 4½" (6.5 × 11.5 cm) *(fig. 5)* and sew them together.

7. Sew a yellow/orange unit to each side of the white square 4½" × 4½" (11.5 × 11.5 cm) *(fig. 6)*. This is the middle block row.

8. Sew an aqua/white foundation-pieced unit (made in Step 1) to each side of an orange/yellow unit *(fig. 7)*. These are the top and bottom block rows.

9. Sew together all three rows to complete the block *(fig. 8)*.

MAKE THE DANCING SQUARES QUILT

Materials

All fabric amounts are for 45" (114.5 cm) wide fabric.

- 3 yd (2.75 m) white solid fabric
- ¼ yd (34.5 cm) purple print fabric
- ¼ yd (34.5 cm) hot pink print fabric
- ½ yd (45.5 cm) light green print fabric
- ½ yd (45.5 cm) dark green print fabric
- ⅓ yd (45.5 cm) orange print fabric
- ⅓ yd (30.5 cm) yellow print fabric
- 3¼ yd (2.97m) backing fabric
- 59" × 76" (150 × 193.1 cm) low-loft cotton batting
- ⅝ yd (57 cm) binding fabric

Tools

- Rolling Squares Template*
- Flying Geese Template (optional)
- Foundation-piecing paper

* You will need to print forty-eight copies of the Rolling Squares Template at 100 percent.

Cutting

FROM WHITE SOLID FABRIC, CUT:

- ❑ 96 squares 3½" × 3½" (9 × 9 cm); cut in half diagonally to make 192 half-square triangles.
- ❑ 96 squares 2⅞" × 2⅞" (7.3 × 7.3 cm); cut in half diagonally to make 192 half-square triangles.
- ❑ 56 squares 4½" × 4½" (11.5 × 11.5 cm).
- ❑ 64 rectangles 2½" × 4½" (6.5 × 11.5 cm).

FROM PURPLE PRINT FABRIC, CUT:

- ❑ 24 squares 3½" × 3½" (9 × 9 cm).

FROM HOT PINK PRINT FABRIC, CUT:

- ❑ 24 squares 3½" × 3½" (9 × 9 cm).

FROM LIGHT GREEN PRINT FABRIC, CUT:

- ❑ 12 squares 5¼" × 5¼" (13.5 × 13.5 cm).

FROM DARK GREEN PRINT FABRIC, CUT:

- ❑ 12 squares 5¼" × 5¼" (13.5 × 13.5 cm).

FROM ORANGE PRINT FABRIC, CUT:

- ❑ 32 rectangles 2½" × 4½" (6.5 × 11.5 cm).

FROM YELLOW PRINT FABRIC, CUT:

- ❑ 16 squares 4½" × 4½" (11.5 × 11.5 cm).

FROM BINDING FABRIC, CUT:

- ❑ 7 strips 2½" (6.5 cm) × width of fabric.

Rolling Squares Blocks

UNFINISHED BLOCK: 12½" × 12½" (31.5 × 31.5 cm)

There are three different blocks—A, B, and C. Make eight of block A, twelve of block B, and four of block C.

Block A

1 Follow the Classic Rolling Squares block instructions to foundation-piece sixteen of the purple/white units and sixteen of the pink/white units.

2 Make sixteen light green and sixteen dark green Flying Geese units. To make multiple Flying Geese units, foundation-piece the Flying Geese using the optional template (this method may give you greater accuracy) or use the method shown in the Classic Rolling Squares block instructions. (Fabric requirements listed opposite are for the method described in the Classic block instructions.)

3 Sew together the units to make eight of block A. Make four blocks with the purple units in the upper right and lower left corners of the block and four blocks with the purple units in the upper left and lower right corners.

Block B

1 Make twenty-four light green Flying Geese units and twenty-four dark green units.

2 Match up each completed Flying Geese unit with a white rectangle 2½" × 4½" (6.5 × 11.5 cm) *(fig. 9)* and sew them together. The white rectangle should always be adjoining the green triangle point, as shown.

3 Sew a dark green/white unit to each side of the yellow squares 4½" × 4½" (11.5 × 11.5 cm) for the middle block rows. (You will have some yellow squares left over for Block C). Sew one white square 4½" × 4½" (11.5 × 11.5 cm) to each side of the light green/white units *(fig. 10)* for the top and bottom block rows.

4 Sew together the three rows to create twelve of Block B.

5 Cut three of the B blocks in half diagonally to create setting triangles for the top and bottom of the quilt *(fig. 11)*.

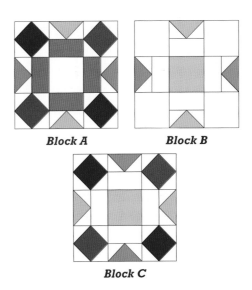

Block A   **Block B**

Block C

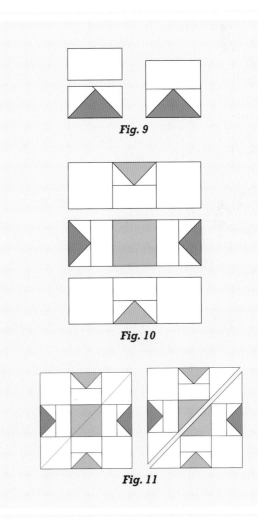

Fig. 9

Fig. 10

Fig. 11

Block C

1 Follow the Classic Rolling Square block instructions, but use the remaining 4½" × 4½" (11.5 × 11.5 cm) yellow squares for the block centers and the remaining 2½" × 4½" (6.5 × 11.5 cm) white rectangles in place of the orange pieces. Make eight foundation-pieced purple/white units and eight foundation-pieced pink/white units.

2 Sew together the units to make four of block C. Make two blocks with the purple units in the upper right and lower left corners of the block and two blocks with the purple units in the upper left and lower right corners *(fig. 12)*.

3 Cut the C blocks in half diagonally to create the eight setting triangles for the sides of the quilt. Note the color positioning *(fig. 13)*.

Quilt Top

1 Arrange the A, B, and C blocks on point, as shown in the Dancing Squares Construction Diagram. Note color positioning in the quilt photo. Sew together the blocks in diagonal rows. Press seams toward the B blocks. Sew together the rows to create a finished quilt top. Press.

2 Make a quilt sandwich with the backing, batting, and quilt top. Baste the layers and quilt as desired. I chose to stitch very clean, simple straight lines. Trim the batting and backing to match the quilt top.

3 Join the binding strips to make a continuous length. Bind the raw edges to finish the quilt.

MINI HISTORY LESSON: *Rolling Stone Blocks and Their Variations*

The Rolling Squares block is a variation on the classic Rolling Stone block, which quilters have been using regularly since the 1800s. Rolling Squares simply adds Flying Geese units to the edges of the block, making it just a bit more angular than its predecessor.

Antique examples of Rolling Stone blocks abound, many dating from the 1870s and 1880s. Along with Rolling Squares and its Flying Geese, other variations of this block included nine-patch formations, star shapes, and more. Also known as the Broken Wheel block, Rolling Stone designs sometimes appeared in signature quilts, which were popular in the mid-1880s. The center of the block was a perfect spot for friends and family members to sign their names. Antique quilts featuring Rolling Stone designs show the blocks set on-point, alternating with solid blocks, or with cornerstones or sashing. Clearly, quilters of the 1800s were as aware of this block's possibilities as are today's quilters.

Fig. 12

Fig. 13

Dancing Squares Construction Diagram

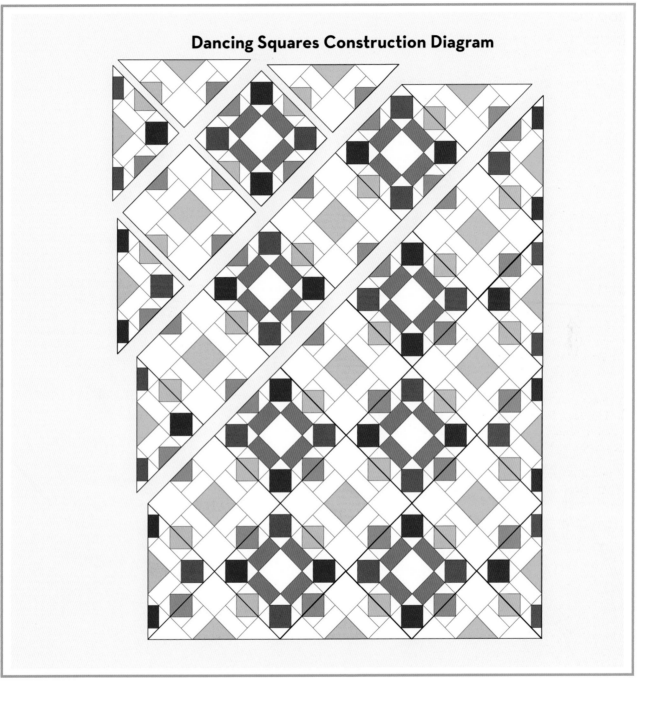

BLOCK:
Red Cross

PROJECT:
Cross Point Quilt

*Designed and made by **Faith Jones***

FINISHED SIZE:	TECHNIQUE USED:	SKILL LEVEL:
60" × 60" (152.5 × 152.5 cm)	Foundation piecing	Intermediate

DESIGN NOTE: | *Placing Blocks and Designs On-Point*

You can change the entire look of a quilt design by rotating blocks 45 degrees to place them "on-point." The movement and dynamics of a design often change radically when setting blocks on-point. One of the best ways to see this design impact is to compare my Sampler Quilt On-Point (page 154) with one of the other two sampler quilts (pages 148 and 150). In the case of the Red Cross quilt block, placing the block on-point changes the design from an "X" to a cross.

Setting an entire collection of blocks on-point—as I did here with the Cross Point Quilt—and placing them exactly in the center of a quilt creates an unexpected but dramatic design. This type of layout, which relates to the medallion quilt, would be perfect for a bed, where the eye focuses on the quilt center.

Faith Jones

CLASSIC RED CROSS BLOCK

UNFINISHED BLOCK: 12½" × 12½" (31.5 × 31.5 cm)

Choose scraps from your stash to make this classic version for a block swap or bee. If you want to make it for a sampler quilt, see pages 146–157. To make the Cross Point Quilt version, see opposite page. Red Cross templates A and B are on the CD included with this book.

Cutting

FROM AQUA FABRIC, CUT:

- ❏ 2 strips 2½" × 7¼" (6.5 × 18.5 cm) (template piece A5).

FROM GREEN FABRIC, CUT:

- ❏ 2 strips 2½" × 7¼" (6.5 × 18.5 cm) (template piece A5).

FROM YELLOW FABRIC, CUT:

- ❏ 4 squares 2¾" × 2¾" (7 × 7 cm) (template pieces A1 and B1).

FROM RED FABRIC, CUT:

- ❏ 4 squares 2¾" × 2¾" (7 × 7 cm) (template piece A1 and B1).

FROM WHITE FABRIC, CUT:

- ❏ 8 squares 4" × 4" (10 × 10 cm); cut in half diagonally to make 16 half-square triangles (template pieces A2, A3, B2, and B3).

- ❏ 8 squares 3" × 3" (7.5 × 7.5 cm); cut in half diagonally to make 16 half-square triangles (template pieces A4, A6, A7, and B4).

Assembling the Block

1. Print and cut out four copies of *each* Red Cross Template at 100 percent.

2. Using the technique described in Guide to Foundation Piecing (page 13), piece eight templates. Use the cutting instructions above to identify which fabric pieces correspond to each template number. For my design, I paired the green fabric with the red fabric and the aqua fabric with the yellow fabric *(fig. 1)*.

3. Lay out the four pieced-block quadrants *(fig. 2)* and sew them together.

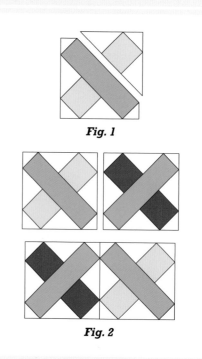

Fig. 1

Fig. 2

MAKE THE CROSS POINT QUILT

Materials

All fabric amounts are for 45" (114.5 cm) wide fabric.

- ⅓ yd (30.5 cm) light blue fabric
- ⅓ yd (30.5 cm) dark blue fabric
- ⅓ yd (30.5 cm) light green fabric
- ⅓ yd (30.5 cm) dark green fabric
- 2½ yd (2.3 m) white fabric
- ⅛ yd 11.5 cm) orange fabric
- 2 yd (1.8 m) gray fabric
- 3½ yd (3.2 m) backing fabric
- 68" × 68" (172.7 × 172.7 cm) low-loft cotton batting
- ⅝ yd (57 cm) binding fabric

Tools

- Red Cross templates A and B*
- Foundation-piecing paper

** You will need to print thirty-six copies of **each** Red Cross Template at 100 percent.*

Cutting

FROM LIGHT BLUE FABRIC, CUT:

❐ 18 strips 2½" × 7¼" (6.5 × 18.5 cm) (template piece A5).

FROM DARK BLUE FABRIC, CUT:

❐ 18 strips 2½" × 7¼" (6.5 × 18.5 cm) (template piece A5).

FROM LIGHT GREEN FABRIC, CUT:

❐ 36 squares 2¾" × 2¾" (7 × 7 cm) (template piece B1).

FROM DARK GREEN FABRIC, CUT:

❐ 36 squares 2¾" × 2¾" (7 × 7 cm) (template piece B1).

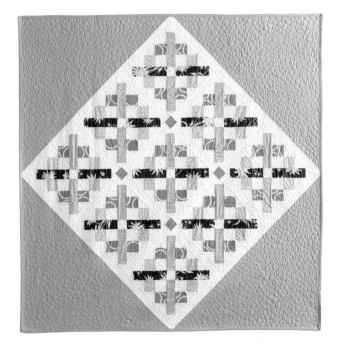

FROM WHITE FABRIC, CUT:

❐ 72 squares 4" × 4" (10 × 10 cm), cut in half diagonally to make 144 half-square triangles (template pieces A2, A3, B2, and B3).

❐ 72 squares 3" × 3" (7.5 × 7.5 cm) , cut in half diagonally to make 144 half-square triangles (template pieces A4, A6, A7, and B4).

❐ 12 strips 2¼" × 12½" (5.5 × 31.5 cm) for sashing.

❐ 2 strips 2¼" × 40" (5.5 × 101.5 cm) for sashing.

❐ 2 strips 2¼" × 43½" (5.5 × 110.5 cm) for sashing.

FROM ORANGE FABRIC, CUT:

❐ 4 squares 2¼" × 2¼" (5.5 × 5.5 cm) (cornerstones).

FROM GRAY FABRIC, CUT:

❐ 2 squares 30" × 30" (76 × 76 cm), cut in half diagonally to make 4 half-square triangles.

FROM BINDING FABRIC, CUT:

❐ 7 strips 2½" (6.5 cm) × width of fabric.

Red Cross Blocks

UNFINISHED BLOCK:
12½" × 12½" (31.5 × 31.5 cm)

Follow the Classic Red Cross block instructions to make nine blocks. Use the cutting instructions to identify which fabric pieces correspond to each template number.

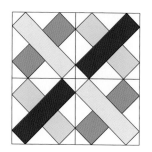

Quilt Top

1 Lay out the blocks in rows of three *(fig. 3)*. Between each block, sew a white rectangle 2¼" × 12½" (5.5 × 31.5 cm).

2 To make a horizontal sashing strip, sew together three white strips 2¼" × 12½" (5.5 × 31.5 cm) and two orange squares 2¼" × 2¼" (5.5 × 5.5 cm) *(fig. 4)*. Make two.

3 Refer to *fig. 5* to lay out the center of the quilt top. Sew together the top row and one sashing strip, then add the middle row, the second sashing strip, and the bottom row.

4 Sew the two white strips 2¼" × 40" (5.5 × 101.5 cm) to the quilt top sides. Sew the two white strips 2¼" × 43½" (5.5 × 110.5 cm) to the top and bottom *(fig. 5)*.

5 Sew the large gray triangles to the corners of the assembled quilt top center as shown in the Cross Point Construction Diagram. The white borders will extend beyond the gray triangles, but you will trim them off in the finishing process.

6 Make a quilt sandwich with the backing, batting, and quilt top. Baste the layers and quilt as desired. I used a pebble design. Trim the batting and backing to match the quilt top. On the quilt top, trim off the white border points even with the quilt edges.

7 Join the binding strips to make a continuous length. Bind the raw edges to finish the quilt.

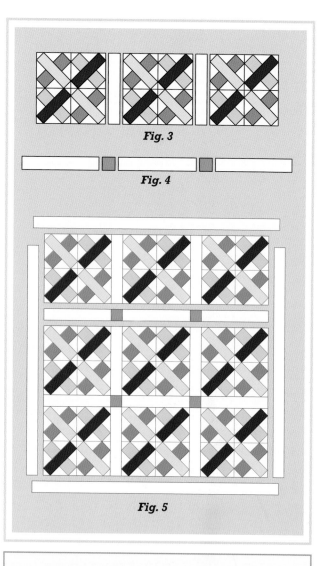

Fig. 3

Fig. 4

Fig. 5

MINI HISTORY LESSON:
Medallion Quilts in America

Medallion quilts—quilts with a central focus surrounded by several borders—were extremely popular in America from the late 1700s to mid 1800s. The central motifs and elaborate borders were designed perfectly for display on beds. It wasn't until the second half of the nineteenth century that the popularity of quilts made from rows of blocks surged, and medallion quilts became less common.

Cross Point Construction Diagram

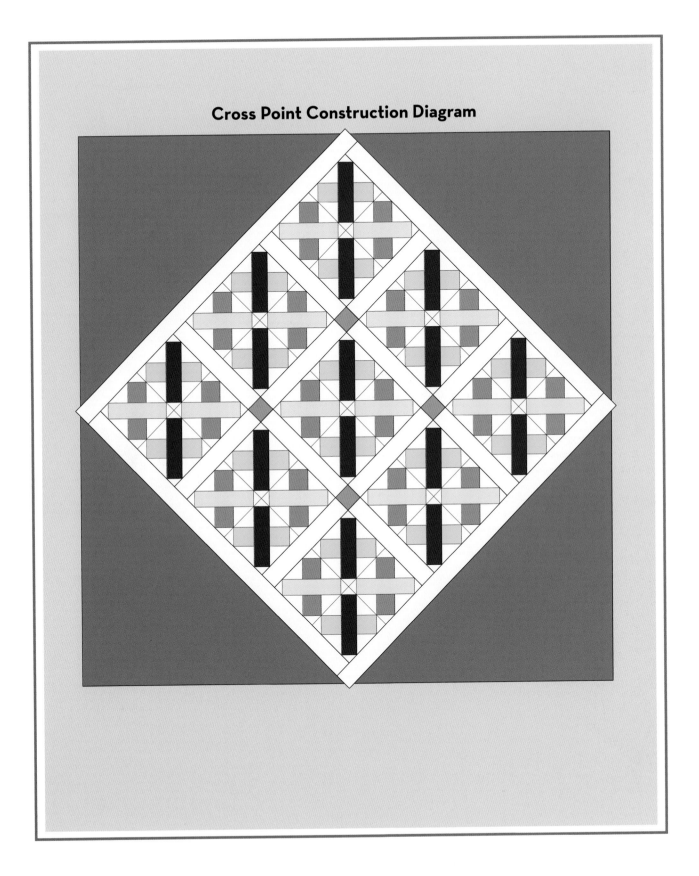

BLOCK:
Mayflower

PROJECT:
New World Pouch

Designed and made by **Katie Clark Blakesley**

FINISHED SIZE:	TECHNIQUES USED:	SKILL LEVEL:
7½" × 10" (19 × 25.5 cm)	Foundation piecing, zipper installation	Intermediate

DESIGN NOTE:	*Changing Block Size*

Patchwork can be used for more than just quilts—pillows, bags, aprons, pot holders, pincushions, zippered pouches, and more are all perfect destinations for pieced blocks. The New World Pouch mixes a linen/cotton blend with prints and solids in a monochromatic color scheme. Projects like this pouch are a great place to add a bit of your favorite fabrics—the addition of the white text print adds flair to the simple color palette. Here, the unfinished Mayflower block is sized down dramatically to 3" × 3" (7.5 × 7.5 cm). Miniature piecing can help you improve your accuracy, as well as add a focal point to your sewn projects.

Patchwork projects are also a great opportunity to experiment with changing the size of your quilt blocks. A block that might seem fussy or overdone when repeated in a quilt may be striking in a project with a large single block. Conversely, the repetition of a very simple block, such as the Mayflower block, may be more pleasing to the eye than a single large block.

Katie Clark Blakesley

Classic Mayflower Block

UNFINISHED BLOCK: 12½" × 12½" (31.5 × 31.5 cm)

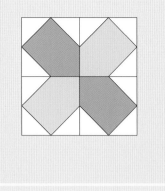

Select two fabrics from your stash to make the classic version for a block swap or bee. If you want to make it for a sampler quilt, see pages 146–157. Use the Mayflower block template on the CD included with this book for the full-size Mayflower block. To make the New World Pouch version, see opposite page.

Cutting

FROM GREEN FABRIC, CUT:

- ☐ 2 rectangles 5" × 7¼" (12.5 × 18.5 cm) (template piece 1).

FROM YELLOW FABRIC, CUT:

- ☐ 2 rectangles 5" × 7¼" (12.5 × 18.5 cm) (template piece 1).

FROM WHITE FABRIC, CUT:

- ☐ 6 squares 4½" × 4½" (11.5 × 11.5 cm); cut in half diagonally to make 12 half-square triangles (template pieces 2, 3, and 4).

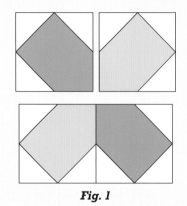

Fig. 1

Assembling the Block

1. Print and cut out four copies of Mayflower Block Template A at 100 percent.

2. Using the technique described in Guide to Foundation Piecing (page 13), piece four templates. Use the cutting instructions above to identify which fabric pieces correspond to each template number.

3. Lay out the four pieced units as shown *(fig. 1)*. Sew together the top two pieces and the bottom two pieces. Press the seams open to reduce bulk. Sew together the block halves.

MAKE THE NEW WORLD POUCH

Materials

All fabric amounts are for 45" (114.5 cm) wide fabric.

- Assorted light and dark scraps at least 2" × 3" (5 cm × 7.5 cm)

- ½ yd (45.5 cm) linen/cotton blend

- 1 fat quarter (18" × 22") (45.5 × 56 cm) lining fabric

- ¼ yd (23 cm) medium-weight fusible interfacing

- 9" (23 cm) zipper

Tools

- Mini Mayflower Pouch Template*

- Foundation-piecing paper

- Zipper foot (optional)

* You will need to print and cut out sixteen copies of the Mini Mayflower Pouch Template at 100 percent.

Cutting

FROM LIGHT SCRAPS, CUT:

- ❒ 8 squares 2" × 2" (5 × 5 cm) (template piece 1).

FROM DARK SCRAPS, CUT:

- ❒ 8 squares 2" × 2" (5 × 5 cm) (template piece 1).

- ❒ 2 rectangles 1½" × 3" (3.8 × 7.5 cm) for zipper tabs.

FROM LINEN/COTTON BLEND, CUT:

- ❒ 48 squares 2" × 2" (5 × 5 cm) (template pieces 2, 3, and 4).

- ❒ 2 rectangles 2½" × 5½" (6.5 × 14 cm).

- ❒ 1 rectangle 2½" × 9½" (6.5 × 24 cm).

- ❒ 1 rectangle 4" × 9½" (10 × 24 cm).

- ❒ 1 rectangle 8" × 10½" (20.5 × 26.5 cm).

FROM INTERFACING, CUT:

- ❒ 2 rectangles 8" × 10½" (20.5 × 26.5 cm).

FROM LINING FABRIC, CUT:

- ❒ 2 rectangles 8" × 10½" (20.5 × 26.5 cm).

Mini Mayflower Blocks

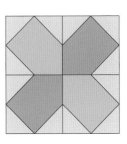

UNFINISHED BLOCK:
3" × 3" (7.5 × 7.5 cm)

1 Follow the Classic Mayflower block instructions to make four mini blocks. Use the cutting instructions to identify which fabric pieces correspond to each template number. Vary the placement of fabric lights and darks as desired.

2 Sew the four blocks together (*fig. 2*).

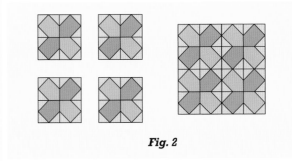

Fig. 2

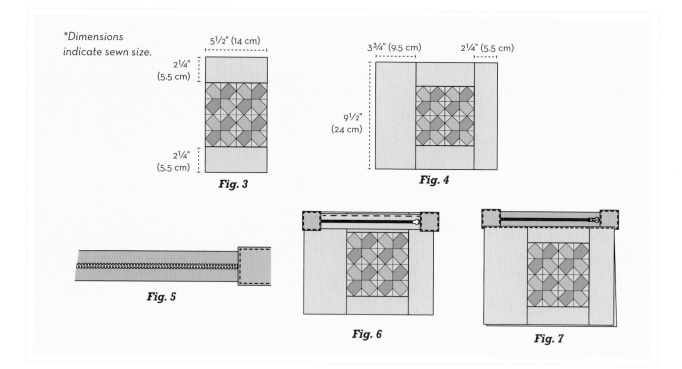

*Dimensions indicate sewn size.

Fig. 3

Fig. 4

Fig. 5

Fig. 6

Fig. 7

Pouch Construction

1 To assemble the front of the pouch, refer to *fig. 3* to sew one linen/cotton rectangle 2½" × 5½" (6.5 × 14 cm) to the top and the bottom of the four-patch square. Press. Sew the linen/cotton rectangle 2½" × 9½" (6.5 × 24 cm) to the right edge of the four-patch block and the linen/cotton rectangle 4" × 9½" (10 × 24 cm) to the left edge *(fig. 4)*. Press. Trim the pouch front to 8" × 10½" (20.5 × 26.5 cm).

2 Follow the manufacturer's directions to fuse the interfacing to the wrong sides of the 8" × 10½" (20.5 × 26.5 cm) pouch front and the back pouch rectangles.

3 Covering the ends of the zipper with fabric tabs makes the pouch more finished and is a simple way to add color. Fold the two dark rectangles 1½" × 3" (3.8 × 7.5 cm) in half lengthwise and press. Press long edges in ¼" (6 mm). Encase both zipper ends in a folded rectangle and stitch very close to the edge *(fig. 5)*.

4 Place the closed zipper facedown on the pouch front, with the pull on the right side, lining up the top edge of the zipper tape with the pouch front top edge. **Note:** *The zipper tabs will extend slightly beyond the pouch front edges.* Baste in place close to the zipper tape edge *(fig. 6)*.

5 Place one lining rectangle 8" × 10½" (20.5 × 26.5 cm) on top of the pouch front, right sides together, aligning the top edges and sandwiching the zipper between. Pin in place.

6 Using a zipper foot, adjust the needle position to stitch just inside the basting line. Start stitching at the bottom of the zipper and stop 3" (7.5 cm) from the zipper pull. Raise the foot and, with the needle in the down position, unzip the zipper to make it easier to complete the seam.

7 Fold the pouch front and the lining away from the zipper, wrong sides together. Carefully press the seam. Avoid having the iron touch the zipper coils.

8 With the lining and pouch front pulled away from the zipper, topstitch the seam through all layers *(fig. 7)*.

9 Lay the pouch front right side up and place the pouch back on top, right sides together, lining up the pouch back top edge with the edge of the zipper tape. Baste in place close to the zipper tape edge.

10 Pin the lining rectangle 8" × 10½" (20.5 × 26.5 cm) under the pouch front/lining, with the lining rectangles right sides together. Line up the top lining edge with the zipper tape edge.

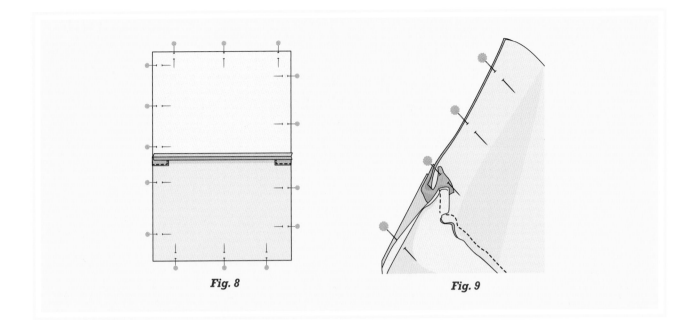

Fig. 8   Fig. 9

11 Sew in place, repeating Steps 6 to 8.

12 Open the zipper at least halfway. Fold back the lining and pouch rectangles separately, placing both right sides together. Trim the zipper tab length if needed (*fig 8*).

13 Pin the zipper tabs toward the lining on both sides of the pouch (*fig. 9*).

14 Using a generous ¼" (6 cm) seam, sew all around the pouch edges, stitching slowly over the bulky zipper tabs. Leave a 3" (7.5 cm) opening in the lining bottom for turning. Trim the corners.

15 Turn the pouch right side out through the lining and zipper openings. Poke out the square corners using a chopstick or point turner. Handstitch the lining opening closed.

Note: *Don't sew over a zipper with metal teeth; your needle will break! Instead, sew very slowly just up to the zipper and backstitch. Then backstitch just on the other side of the zipper and continue stitching.*

MINI HISTORY LESSON:
Renaming Quilt Blocks for Cultural Relevance

Today, as in the past, quilt blocks often get renamed to fit the times. According to Barbara Brackman's *Encyclopedia of Pieced Quilt Patterns,* the early name "Mayflower" for this quilt block is referenced as Pattern No. 200 of the Ladies Art Company, the first U.S. mail-order pattern business. (For more about the LAC, see page 116.) This traditional name evoked the history of the pilgrims who sailed to the New World on the Mayflower in the 1600s. But in 1934, Nancy Cabot, who published a newspaper column in the *Chicago Daily Tribune,* printed a slightly stylized version of the block, which she referred to by the name "Hard Times." Cabot noted in her article that the block was enjoying newfound popularity. During the Great Depression, no doubt the name Hard Times had something to do with its relevance and popularity. Cabot sometimes sold templates of blocks printed in her newspaper columns; she sold Hard Times for 5 cents per template.

BLOCK:
Tea Leaf

PROJECT:
Spiced Chai Quilt

Designed and made by **Katie Clark Blakesley**

FINISHED SIZE:	**TECHNIQUE USED:**	**SKILL LEVEL:**
60" × 60" (152.5 × 152.5 cm)	Simple piecing	Beginner

DESIGN NOTE:	*Altering a Traditional Block Layout*

A striking quilt often starts with a great block that is used in an interesting or unexpected way. Traditionally, a full quilt of Tea Leaf blocks would start with a standard quilt layout of repeating blocks set in a grid with sashing between them.

In this case, a few key design changes—eliminating the sashing, using a larger than standard 12½" (31.5 cm) size block, and rotating several of the blocks so they aren't all facing the same direction—update this quilt for the twenty-first century.

Adding to a more contemporary look is the use of a neutral color palette. The twelve "background" Tea Leaf blocks are sewn with white fabric and varying shades of gray solids. A couple of key "pops" of bold color—including the single large Tea Leaf Star block—create dramatic focal points.

The Spiced Chai quilt and Tea Leaf block lend themselves well to experimenting with block layout. Try "floating" the Tea Leaf Star in negative space by piecing only the four colored blocks. Or, supersize the Tea Leaf Star or a single Tea Leaf block for a baby quilt that has an entirely new look.

Katie Clark Blakesley

CLASSIC TEA LEAF BLOCK

UNFINISHED BLOCK: 12½" × 12½" (31.5 × 31.5 cm)

Choose scraps from your stash to make this classic version for a block swap or bee. If you want to make it for a sampler quilt, see pages 146–157. To make the Spiced Chai Quilt version, see opposite page.

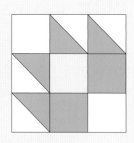

Cutting

FROM WHITE FABRIC, CUT:

☐ 2 squares 4½" × 4½" (11.5 × 11.5 cm).

☐ 2 squares 5¼" × 5¼" (13.5 × 13.5 cm).

FROM AQUA FABRIC, CUT:

☐ 2 squares 4½" × 4½" (11.5 × 11.5 cm).

FROM GREEN FABRIC, CUT:

☐ 2 squares 5¼" × 5¼" (13.5 × 13.5 cm).

FROM CREAM FABRIC, CUT:

☐ 1 square 4½" × 4½" (11.5 × 11.5 cm).

Assembling the Block

1. To make half-square-triangle units, use a water-soluble pen or other fabric marker to draw a diagonal line from corner to corner on each white square 5¼" × 5¼" (13.5 × 13.5 cm). Match each white square with a green square 5¼" × 5¼" (13.5 ×13.5 cm).

2. Sew a ¼" (6 mm) seam allowance on both sides of the drawn line for both pairs of squares *(fig. 1)*.

3. Cut each square in half diagonally on the drawn line to make two half-square triangle pairs. Open and press the seams toward the darker fabric.

Align the 45-degree ruler marking with the seam and trim the four half-square triangles to 4½" × 4½" (11.5 × 11.5 cm) square.

4. Lay out the white, aqua, and cream 4½" × 4½" (11.5 × 11.5 cm) squares and the half-square triangles in rows *(fig. 2)*. Sew together the squares in three vertical rows and then sew the columns together. Press the seams for each row in alternating directions to nest the seams and make the blocks lie flat.

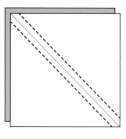

Fig. 1

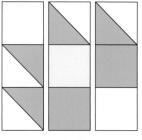

Fig. 2

MAKE THE SPICED CHAI QUILT

Materials

All fabric amounts are for 45" (114.5 cm) wide fabric.

• 2 yd (1.8 m) white fabric

• 2 yd (1.8 m) *total* gray solid fabrics in various shades (see Cutting note)

• 1 fat quarter (18" × 22") (45.5 × 56 cm) each of citron, plum, jade, and orange fabrics, or equivalent scraps*

• 3⅞ yd (3.54 m) backing fabric

• 68" × 68" (172.7 × 172.7 cm) low-loft cotton batting

• ⅝ yd (57 cm) binding fabric

* Use solids, tone-on-tone prints, or color-plus-white prints for maximum impact.

Tools

Water-soluble pen or other fabric marker

Cutting

FROM WHITE FABRIC, CUT:

❏ 1 square 10½" × 10½" (26.5 × 26.5 cm) (Cut this first!).

❏ 28 squares 5½" × 5½" (14 × 14 cm).

❏ 32 squares 6¼" × 6¼" (16 × 16 cm).

FROM GRAY SOLIDS (VARYING SHADES), CUT:

❏ 33 squares 5½" × 5½" total (14 × 14 cm).

❏ 22 squares 6¼" × 6¼" (16 × 16 cm) total.

Note: *To create a block, cut three squares 5½" × 5½" (14 × 14 cm) and two squares 6¼" × 6 ¼" (16 × 16 cm) from the same gray fabric.*

FROM COLORED FABRICS, CUT:

❏ 15 squares 5½" × 5½" (14 × 14 cm) (3 each of citron, jade, and orange; 6 of plum).

❏ 10 squares 6¼" × 6¼" (16 × 16 cm) (2 each of citron, jade, and orange; 4 of plum).

FROM BINDING FABRIC, CUT:

❏ 7 strips 2½" (6.5 cm) × width of fabric.

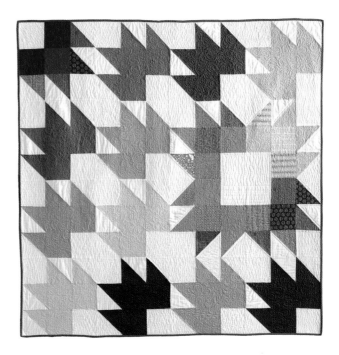

Blocks

This quilt top is made up of twelve Tea Leaf blocks and one large Tea Leaf Star block.

Tea Leaf blocks

UNFINISHED BLOCK:
15½" × 15½" (39.5 × 39.5 cm)

Make twelve blocks.

Eleven of the Tea Leaf blocks are white/gray, and one is white/ bold colored. Follow the Classic Tea Leaf block instructions for creating the half-square-triangle units and assembling the blocks. The blocks for this quilt are 15½" × 15½" unfinished, instead of 12½" × 12½" unfinished like the Classic version.

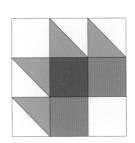

1 Use a water-soluble pen or other fabric marker to draw a diagonal line from corner to corner on the thirty-two white squares 6¼" × 6¼" (16 × 16 cm).

2 Make forty-four half-square triangles using twenty-two white squares 6¼" × 6¼" (16 × 16 cm) and twenty-two gray squares 6¼" × 6¼" (16 × 16 cm). Align a 45-degree ruler line with the seam and trim to 5½" × 5½" (14 × 14 cm) square.

3 Lay out four matching half-square-triangle units, two white squares, and three matching gray squares to make a block, and sew them together like the Classic Tea Leaf block. Make eleven assorted gray blocks.

4 For the white/bold-colored blocks, make twenty half-square-triangle units using the ten remaining white squares 6¼" × 6¼" (16 × 16 cm) and ten bold-colored squares 6¼" × 6¼" (16 × 16 cm). Align a 45-degree ruler line with the seam and trim to 5½" × 5½" (14 × 14 cm) square. Set aside sixteen half-square triangles to use in the Tea Leaf Star block.

5 Lay out the remaining four half-square-triangle units, two white squares, and three bold-colored squares to make a block, and sew them together as for the Classic Tea Leaf block.

Tea Leaf Star Block

UNFINISHED BLOCK: 30½" × 30½" (77.5 × 77.5 cm)

The Tea Leaf Star is an extra-large Nine Patch block; eight of the units are comprised of four squares (two white/bold-colored half-square-triangle units and two squares) with the white 10½" × 10½" (26.5 × 26.5 cm) square in the middle. Some of the units are rotated to create the star pattern.

1 Lay out the sixteen white- and bold-colored half-square-triangle units and the white- and bold-colored squares as shown *(fig. 3)*, with the white square 10½" × 10½" (26.5 × 26.5 cm) in the center. Sew together each of the surrounding eight blocks, pressing seams as you go.

2 Sew and press the blocks together in vertical rows as for the Tea Leaf block. Sew together the three columns and press.

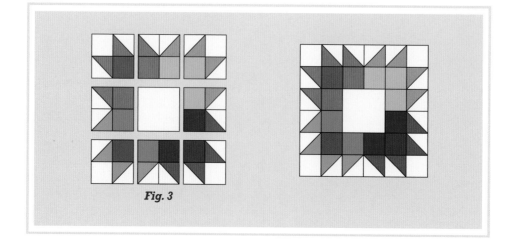

Fig. 3

Spiced Chai Construction Diagram

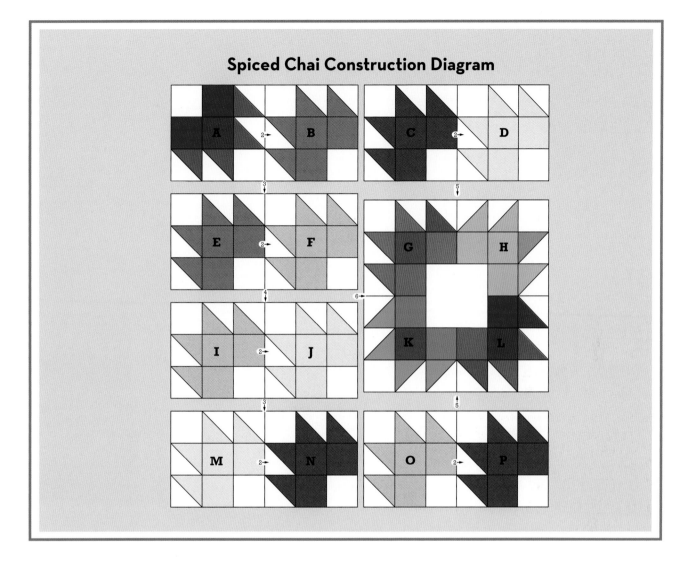

Quilt Top

1 Lay out the blocks as shown in the Spiced Chai Construction Diagram. All white-and-gray blocks face the same direction. Place the white- and bold-colored block in the upper left-hand corner and turn it 180 degrees as shown.

2 Sew together blocks A to B, C to D, E to F, I to J, M to N, and O to P. Press.

3 Sew AB to EF and IJ to MN. Press.

4 Sew ABEF to IJMN. Press.

5 Sew CD to the top of the Tea Leaf Star block and OP to the bottom edge. Press.

6 Sew together the two quilt halves. Press.

7 Make a quilt sandwich with the backing, batting, and quilt top. Baste the layers and quilt as desired. I quilted a fun combination of free-motion designs on this quilt. Trim the batting and backing to match the quilt top.

8 Join the binding strips to make a continuous length. Bind the raw edges to finish the quilt.

BLOCK:
Crosspatch

PROJECT:
Crosspatch Bag

Designed and made by **Lee Heinrich**

FINISHED SIZE:	TECHNIQUE USED:	SKILL LEVEL:
12" × 15" (30.5 × 38 cm)	Foundation piecing	Intermediate

DESIGN NOTE: | *Incorporating Traditional Blocks into Everyday Items*

Quilt blocks aren't just for quilts anymore. Quilters are now incorporating traditional blocks into a variety of everyday accessories and household items, from bags and zipper pouches to pillows and sewing machine covers.

But centering a quilt block on a tote bag isn't the only option. In the Crosspatch Bag, joining Crosspatch blocks into a "custom fabric" for the bag exterior gives it a plaid look.

Applying modern quilting design concepts to non-quilt items is another way to add interest to your projects. Try arranging blocks off-center on a zipper pouch, add negative space to a pieced pillow, make an improvisational version of a traditional block into a fabric journal cover, or add colorful handquilting to a table runner.

CLASSIC CROSSPATCH BLOCK

UNFINISHED BLOCK:
12½" × 12½" (31.5 × 31.5 cm)

Choose scraps from your stash to make this classic version for a block swap or bee. If you want to make it for a sampler quilt, see pages 146–157. To make the Crosspatch Bag version, see opposite page. Crosspatch Block Templates A and B are on the CD included with this book. (Note that these are larger than the Crosspatch Bag Block Templates.)

Cutting

FROM WHITE FABRIC, CUT:

❏ 4 rectangles 3" × 4¼" (7.5 × 11 cm) (template pieces A1 and B1).

❏ 2 squares 2¾" × 2¾" (7 × 7 cm).

❏ 1 strip 2¾" × 7¼" (7 × 18.5 cm).

FROM YELLOW FABRIC, CUT:

❏ 2 squares 3¾" × 3¾" (9.5 × 9.5 cm); cut in half diagonally to make 4 half-square triangles (template pieces A2 and A3).

FROM GREEN FABRIC, CUT:

❏ 2 squares 3¾" × 3¾" (9.5 × 9.5 cm); cut in half diagonally to make 4 half-square triangles (template pieces B2 and B3).

FROM CREAM FABRIC, CUT:

❏ 4 strips 3" × 8" (7.5 × 20.5 cm) (template pieces A4 and B4).

FROM AQUA FABRIC, CUT:

❏ 2 squares 3¼" × 3¼" (8.5 × 8.5 cm); cut in half diagonally to make 4 half-square triangles (template pieces B5 and B6).

FROM ORANGE FABRIC, CUT:

❏ 4 squares 2¾" × 2¾" (7 × 7 cm).

Assembling the Block

1. Print and cut out two copies of *each* Crosspatch Block Template at 100 percent.

2. Using the technique described in Guide to Foundation Piecing (page 13), piece four templates. Use the cutting instructions above to identify which fabric pieces correspond to each template number.

3. To make the block center, sew an orange square 2¾" × 2¾" (7 × 7 cm) to each side of the two white squares 2¾" × 2¾" (7 × 7 cm). Sew an orange-and-white pieced unit to each long edge of the white rectangle 2¾" × 7¼" (7 × 18.5 cm) *(fig. 1)*. Press.

4. Sew one pieced unit A to the right side of the orange-and-white center section. Sew the other pieced unit A to the left side of the center section. Press the seams toward the center. Sew one pieced unit B to the top of the center section and the other pieced unit B to the bottom of the center section *(fig. 2)*. Press.

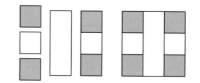

Fig. 1

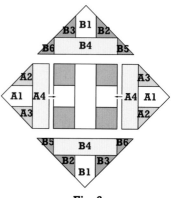

Fig. 2

MAKE THE CROSSPATCH BAG

Materials

All fabric amounts are for 45" (114.5 cm) wide fabric.

- ³/₈ yd (34.5 cm) white fabric
- ³/₈ yd (34.5 cm) dark gray fabric
- ³/₈ yd (34.5 cm) light gray fabric
- ¹/₈ yd (11.5 cm) dark yellow fabric
- ³/₄ yd (68.5 cm) bright yellow fabric
- 1 yd (91.5 cm) medium-weight sew-in interfacing

Tools

- Crosspatch Bag Block Templates A and B*
- Foundation-piecing paper
- Walking foot for sewing machine

** You will need to print sixteen copies of **each** Crosspatch Bag Block Template at 100 percent.*

Cutting

FROM WHITE FABRIC, CUT:

- ☐ 32 rectangles 2¹/₂" × 3¹/₄" (6.5 × 8.5 cm) (template pieces A1 and B1).
- ☐ 8 strips 1¹/₂" × 5" (3.8 × 12.5 cm) (center section).
- ☐ 16 squares 1¹/₂" × 1¹/₂" (3.8 × 3.8 cm) (center section).

FROM DARK GRAY FABRIC, CUT:

- ☐ 32 squares 3" × 3" (7.5 × 7.5 cm), cut in half diagonally to make 64 half-square triangles (template pieces A2, A3, B2, and B3).

FROM LIGHT GRAY FABRIC, CUT:

- ☐ 32 squares 1¹/₂" × 1¹/₂" (3.8 × 3.8 cm) (center section).
- ☐ 2 strips 4" × 21¹/₂" (10 × 54.5 cm) (handles).

FROM DARK YELLOW FABRIC, CUT:

- ☐ 16 squares 2¹/₂" × 2¹/₂" (6.5 × 6.5 cm), cut in half diagonally to make 32 half-square triangles (template pieces B5 and B6).

FROM BRIGHT YELLOW FABRIC, CUT:

- ☐ 32 strips 2¹/₄" × 5³/₄" (5.5 × 14.5 cm) (template pieces A4 and B4).
- ☐ 2 rectangles 13" × 16" (33 × 40.5 cm) (lining).

FROM INTERFACING, CUT:

- ☐ 2 strips 2" × 21¹/₂" (5 × 54.5 cm) (handles).

- ☐ 2 rectangles 13" × 16" (33 × 40.5 cm) (bag body).

Crosspatch Bag Blocks

UNFINISHED BLOCK:
8¹/₂" × 8¹/₂" (21.5 × 21.5 cm)

The block for this bag is made in the same way as the Classic Crosspatch block, but it is smaller. Be sure you are using the Crosspatch Bag templates and not the Crosspatch Block templates!

1 Using the technique described in Guide to Foundation Piecing (page 13), piece thirty-two templates. Use the cutting instructions to identify which fabric pieces correspond to each template number.

2 Sew together the blocks in groups of four to make two units measuring 16½" × 16½" (42 × 42 cm).

3 Trim each of the two block units to 16" wide × 13" tall (40.5 × 33 cm). Be sure to measure from the middle so that the pieced plaid pattern remains centered *(fig. 3)*. These pieced units are the bag front and back.

Bag Construction

1 Place one interfacing rectangle 13" × 16" (33 × 40.5 cm) on the back of the pieced bag front and back, with edges aligned. Using a walking foot, topstitch the pieced sections ⅛" (3 mm) from the ditch *(fig. 4)*. This adds a decorative finish and permanently affixes the bag outer fabric to the interfacing.

2 Place the bag front and back right sides together and sew the two short sides and one long side ¼" (6 mm) from the edge.

3 Repeat Step 2 with the two bright yellow lining rectangles 13" × 16" leaving a 4" (10 cm) opening along the long side for turning.

4 To create a flat bag bottom, fold one bottom corner of the outer bag together so that the side seam and bottom seam meet.

Tip
As I'm folding the corner together, I push the side seam allowance in one direction and the bottom seam allowance in the opposite direction. This allows me to nest the seams together just like in quilting, so the side and bottom seams will line up nicely.

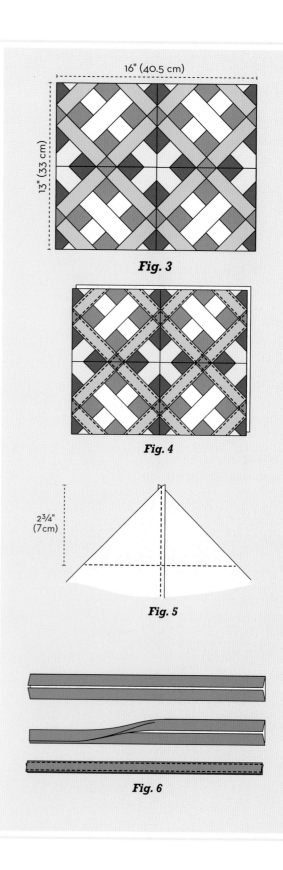

16" (40.5 cm)

13" (33 cm)

Fig. 3

Fig. 4

2¾" (7cm)

Fig. 5

Fig. 6

5 Mark a line across the corner, perpendicular to the seams, 2¾" (7 cm) from the corner point. Stitch along this line, backstitching at the beginning and end of the seams *(fig. 5)*. Trim the seam to ¼" (6 mm).

6 Repeat Steps 4 and 5 with the other bag corner and both lining corners.

7 Press a light gray rectangle 4" × 21½" (10 × 53.5 cm) in half lengthwise. Open the piece flat and then press each long edge inward, meeting the center crease *(fig. 6)*. Open again and center an interfacing strip 2" × 21½" (5 × 54.5 cm) between the folds. Fold the edges back in to completely cover the interfacing and press the strip in half lengthwise to create a 1" (2.5 cm) wide handle. Edgestitch the handle. Make two.

8 Mark 3½" (9 cm) in from each side seam at the bag top edge.

9 With the outer bag wrong side out, place the lining inside with right sides together and raw edges aligned.

10 Place the handles between the outer bag and the lining, with the handle raw edges aligned with the bag top edges and the handle facing down. The outer edges of the handles should be lined up with the marks from Step 8. Pin all around the top edge of the bag.

Tip
Baste the ends of the handles in place ⅛" (3 mm) from the top bag edge.

11 Sew around the top edge of the bag, ½" (1.3 cm) from the raw edges.

12 Turn the bag right side out through the opening. Handstitch the lining opening closed and push the lining down inside the bag.

13 Topstitch around the top edge of the bag ¼" (6 mm) from the edge. Press.

MINI HISTORY LESSON: *Feed Sacks*

The idea of decorative bags goes back a long time and has some humble origins.

According to author Barbara Brackman, in *Making History: Quilts and Fabric from 1890–1970*, feed sacks—which contained flour, sugar, grain, and the like—were initially made of plain white cotton in the late 1800s. They were usually printed only with the product's brand name. But by the 1930s, paper packaging was starting to compete with fabric bags. In response, manufacturers began printing colorful designs on the bags and promoting their use in sewing—a marketing strategy that played well during the Great Depression.

Over the years, feed sacks were used to make everything from clothing and toys to bedding and curtains. Some bags even came with pre-printed sewing or quilt patterns. Using feed sacks in sewing remained popular through the Great Depression and World War II.

Today, some wildly popular modern fabric lines owe much to those printed feed sacks that farmers' wives used in quilts nearly a century ago.

BLOCK:
Star-and-Pinwheel

PROJECT:
Sugar Snow Quilt

*Designed and made by **Lee Heinrich***
*Quilted by **Krista Withers***

FINISHED SIZE:	TECHNIQUE USED:	SKILL LEVEL:
60" × 76" (152.5 × 193 cm)	Simple piecing	Advanced

DESIGN NOTE: | *Finding Design Inspiration*

Many modern quilters find design inspiration in architecture, nature, and the world around them. This quilt is a perfect example of how the natural world inspired me to create a design that goes beyond a traditional grid of repeating quilt blocks.

Around the time I was designing this quilt, I spent an afternoon at my daughter's preschool, which is also a nature center and a working maple-sugar farm. I went with the class to tap a maple tree. While there, a teacher scooped up a handful of the icy, crystalline flakes called "sugar snow," which indicate that it's time to tap the trees. As the light caught the snow, it hit me: I wanted to make a quilt that "sparkled" like that snow.

I varied the size of the Star-and-Pinwheel blocks and gave them a flowing, dynamic layout, creating the impression of snowflakes floating down. The icy blues and golden yellows are meant to evoke the ice crystals, the blue sky, and the sun. I chose natural linen as the background to give the whole thing a textured, homespun look that's, well, natural.

CLASSIC STAR-AND-PINWHEEL BLOCK

UNFINISHED BLOCK: 12½" × 12½" (31.5 × 31.5 cm)

In this block, the pinwheel forms the center of a larger star created by adding Flying Geese units. Choose scraps from your stash to make this classic version for a block swap or bee. If you want to make it for a sampler quilt, see pages 146–157. To make the Sugar Snow Quilt version, see page 66.

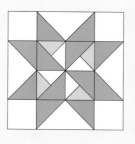

Cutting

FROM GREEN FABRIC, CUT:

❐ 2 squares 3⅞" × 3⅞" (9.75 × 9.75 cm); cut in half diagonally to make 4 half-square triangles.

❐ 2 squares 4¼" × 4¼" (11 × 11 cm); cut in half diagonally to make 4 half-square triangles.

FROM AQUA FABRIC, CUT:

❐ 2 squares 3⅞" × 3⅞" (9.75 × 9.75 cm); cut in half diagonally to make 4 half-square triangles.

FROM YELLOW FABRIC, CUT:

❐ 1 square 4½" × 4½" (11.5 × 11.5 cm).

FROM WHITE FABRIC, CUT:

❐ 1 square 4½" × 4½" (11.5 × 11.5 cm).

❐ 1 square 7¼" × 7¼" (18.5 × 18.5 cm).

❐ 4 squares 3½" × 3½" (9 × 9 cm).

Assembling the Block

1. To make the pinwheel, cut the white and the yellow squares 4½" × 4½" (11.5 × 11.5 cm) in half diagonally twice, to create four quarter-square triangles from each square *(fig. 1)*.

2. Sew each white triangle to a yellow triangle along one short edge, with the white triangle always on the right *(fig. 2)*. Make four white-and-yellow triangle units. Press the seams open.

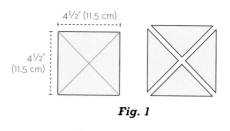

4½" (11.5 cm)

4½" (11.5 cm)

Fig. 1

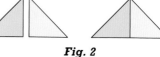

Fig. 2

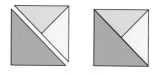

Fig. 3

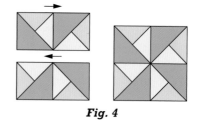

Fig. 4

7¼" (18.5 cm)

7¼" (18.5 cm)

Fig. 5

3. Sew each white-and-yellow unit to a green 4¼" (11 cm) half-square triangle along the diagonal edge as shown *(fig. 3)*, creating four green/white/yellow units. Press the seams toward the green fabric.

4. Note the center point of each unit (where the two angled seams come together). With a 45-degree ruler marking aligned with the center angled seam, trim each edge of the unit 1¾" from the center point. Trimmed units should measure 3½" × 3½" (9 × 9 cm) square.

5. Sew the green/white/yellow units together to create a double pinwheel, pressing seams in the direction of the arrows *(fig. 4)*. Position the units so that the white triangles are toward the inside of the pinwheel.

6. To make the Flying Geese units, cut the white square 7¼" × 7¼" (18.5 × 18.5 cm) in half diagonally twice, to create four quarter-square triangles *(fig. 5)*.

7. Sew a green 3⅞" (9.75 cm) half-square triangle to the left edge of a white quarter-square triangle, right sides together *(fig. 6)*. Make sure the bottom edges of the green half-square triangle and the white triangle are aligned and that the green half-square triangle is always sewn onto the left side of the triangle.

8. Repeat Step 7 with an aqua half-square triangle on the right edge of the white triangle to complete the Flying Geese unit *(fig. 7)*. Press the seams open. The unit should now be 3½" × 6½" (9 × 16.5 cm) *(fig. 8)*.

9. Repeat Steps 7 and 8 with the remaining white quarter-square triangles and the green and aqua half-square triangles to make a total of four Flying Geese units.

10. Sew a Flying Geese unit to each side of the pinwheel unit as shown, pressing seams in the direction of the arrows *(fig. 9)*.

11. Sew a 3½" × 3½" (9 × 9 cm) white square to each side of the remaining two Flying Geese units, pressing seams in the direction of the arrows *(fig. 10)*.

12. Sew together the three rows as shown *(fig. 11)*.

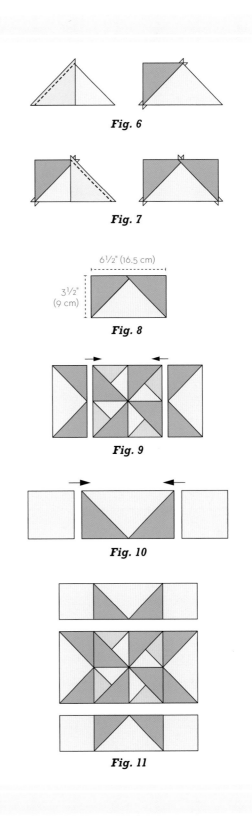

Fig. 6

Fig. 7

6½" (16.5 cm)

3½" (9 cm)

Fig. 8

Fig. 9

Fig. 10

Fig. 11

MAKE THE SUGAR SNOW QUILT

Materials

All fabric amounts are for 45" (114.5 cm) wide fabric.

- ³⁄₄ yd (68.5 cm) teal print fabric
- ¹⁄₂ yd (45.5 cm) light blue print fabric
- ¹⁄₄ yd (23 cm) white print fabric
- ¹⁄₄ yd (23 cm) gold print fabric
- 3¹⁄₂ yd (3.2 m) natural linen
- 3⁷⁄₈ yd (3.54 m) backing fabric
- 68" × 84" (172.7 × 213.4 cm) low-loft cotton batting
- ³⁄₄ yd (68.5 cm) binding fabric

Cutting

FROM TEAL PRINT FABRIC, CUT:

- ❑ 2 squares 7¹⁄₄" × 7¹⁄₄" (18.5 × 18.5 cm); cut in half diagonally to make 4 half-square triangles

- ❑ 2 squares 6⁷⁄₈" × 6⁷⁄₈" (17.5 × 17.5 cm); cut in half diagonally to make 4 half-square triangles

- ❑ 2 squares 5¹⁄₄" × 5¹⁄₄" (13.5 × 13.5 cm); cut in half diagonally to make 4 half-square triangles

- ❑ 2 squares 4⁷⁄₈" × 4⁷⁄₈" (12.3 × 12.3 cm); cut in half diagonally to make 4 half-square triangles

- ❑ 4 squares 4¹⁄₄" × 4¹⁄₄" (11 × 11 cm); cut in half diagonally to make 8 half-square triangles

- ❑ 4 squares 3⁷⁄₈" × 3⁷⁄₈" (9.75 × 9.75 cm); cut in half diagonally to make 8 half-square triangles

- ❑ 1 square 3¹⁄₂" × 3¹⁄₂" (9 × 9 cm)

- ❑ 10 squares 3¹⁄₄" × 3¹⁄₄" (8.5 × 8.5 cm); cut in half diagonally to make 20 half-square triangles

- ❑ 9 squares 2⁷⁄₈" × 2⁷⁄₈" (7.25 × 7.25 cm); cut in half diagonally to make 18 half-square triangles.

FROM LIGHT BLUE PRINT FABRIC, CUT:

- ❑ 2 squares 6⁷⁄₈" × 6⁷⁄₈" (17.5 × 17.5 cm); cut in half diagonally to make 4 half-square triangles

- ❑ 2 squares 4⁷⁄₈" × 4⁷⁄₈" (12.25 × 12.25 cm); cut in half diagonally to make 4 half-square triangles.

- ❑ 4 squares 3⁷⁄₈" × 3⁷⁄₈" (9.75 × 9.75 cm); cut in half diagonally to make 8 half-square triangles

- ❑ 1 square 3¹⁄₂" × 3¹⁄₂" (9 × 9 cm)

- ❑ 9 squares 2⁷⁄₈" × 2⁷⁄₈" (7.25 × 7.25 cm); cut in half diagonally to make 18 half-square triangles).

FROM WHITE PRINT FABRIC, CUT:

- ❑ 1 square 7¹⁄₂" × 7¹⁄₂" (19 × 19 cm); cut in half twice diagonally to make 4 quarter-square triangles

- ❑ 1 square 5¹⁄₂" × 5¹⁄₂" (14 × 14 cm); cut in half twice diagonally to make 4 quarter-square triangles

- ❑ 2 squares 4¹⁄₂" × 4¹⁄₂" (11.5 × 11.5 cm); cut in half twice diagonally to make 8 quarter-square triangles

- ❑ 5 squares 3¹⁄₂" × 3¹⁄₂" (9 × 9 cm); cut in half twice diagonally to make 20 quarter-square triangles.

FROM GOLD PRINT FABRIC, CUT:

❑ 1 square 7½" × 7½" (19 × 19 cm); cut in half twice diagonally to make 4 quarter-square triangles

❑ 1 square 5½" × 5½" (14 × 14 cm); cut in half twice diagonally to make 4 quarter-square triangles

❑ 2 squares 4½" × 4½" (11.5 × 11.5 cm); cut in half twice diagonally to make 8 quarter-square triangles

❑ 5 squares 3½" × 3½" (9 × 9 cm); cut in half twice diagonally to make 20 quarter-square triangles.

FROM LINEN, CUT THESE PIECES IN ORDER:

❑ 1 strip 24½" (62 cm) × width of fabric; sub-cut to make 1 rectangle 24½" × 36½" (62 × 92.5 cm) and 1 strip 4½" × 24½" (11.5 × 62 cm)

❑ 1 strip 16½" (42 cm) × width of fabric; sub-cut to make 1 square 16½" × 16½" (42 × 42 cm) and 2 rectangles 8½" × 16½"(21.5 × 42 cm)

❑ 1 strip 13¼" (33.5 cm) × width of fabric; sub-cut to make 1 square 13¼" × 13¼" (33.5 × 33.5 cm) and 1 rectangle 12½" × 20½" (31.5 × 52 cm). Cut the 13¼" × 13¼" (33.5 × 33.5 cm) square in half twice diagonally to make 4 quarter-square triangles

❑ 1 strip 12½" (31.5 cm) × width of fabric; sub-cut to make 1 rectangle 12½" × 24½" (31.5 × 62 cm) and 1 square 12½" × 12½" (31.5 × 31.5 cm)

❑ 1 strip 8½" (21.5 cm) × width of fabric; sub-cut to make 1 strip 8½" × 24½" (21.5 × 62 cm) and 1 rectangle 8½" × 12½" (21.5 × 31.5 cm)

❑ 1 strip 8½" (21.5 cm) × width of fabric; sub-cut to make 1 strip 8½" × 24½" (21.5 × 62 cm) and 1 square 8½" × 8½" (21.5 × 21.5 cm).

From remaining linen, cut:

❑ 1 strip 4½" × 40½" (11.5 × 103 cm)

❑ 1 strip 4½" × 20½" (11.5 × 52 cm)

❑ 1 strip 4½" × 12½" (11.5 × 31.5 cm)

❑ 1 square 9¼" × 9¼" (23.5 × 23.5 cm); cut in half twice diagonally to make 4 quarter-square triangles

❑ 2 squares 7¼" × 7¼" (18.5 × 18.5 cm); cut in half twice diagonally to make 8 quarter-square triangles

❑ 4 squares 6½" × 6½" (16.5 × 16.5 cm)

❑ 5 squares 5¼" × 5¼" (13.5 × 13.5 cm); cut in half twice diagonally to make 20 quarter-square triangles

❑ 4 rectangles 4½" × 8½" (11.5 × 21.5 cm)

❑ 5 squares 4½" × 4½" (11.5 × 11.5 cm)

❑ 10 squares 3½" × 3½" (9 × 9 cm)

❑ 20 squares 2½" × 2½" (6.5 × 6.5 cm).

FROM BINDING FABRIC, CUT:

❑ 8 strips 2½" (6.5 cm) × width of fabric.

Star-and-Pinwheel Blocks

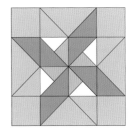

Make whole blocks in four different sizes, plus two half-blocks.

1 Sort the pieces for the blocks into stacks by block size as indicated in the block diagrams on pages 68 and 69. You will have linen pieces remaining; set these aside to use later for assembling the quilt background.

2 Follow the Classic Star-and-Pinwheel block instructions on pages 64–65 to create the blocks. The block instructions are for the 12½" × 12½" (31.5 × 31.5 cm) unfinished block. All other whole blocks are created in the same way, but with different-size pieces. Refer to the block diagrams for fabric sizes and placement.

3 The two half-blocks 4½" × 8½" (11.5 × 21.5 cm) are constructed slightly differently, as shown in the half-block diagram and instructions on page 69.

Whole blocks

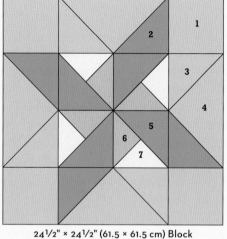

**24½" × 24½" (61.5 × 61.5 cm) Block
Make 1.**

Use:

1. 4 linen squares
   6½" × 6½" (16.5 × 16.5 cm)
2. 4 teal half-square
   triangles 6⅞" (17.5 cm)
3. 4 light blue half-square
   triangles 6⅞" (17.5 cm)
4. 4 linen quarter-square
   triangles 13¼" (33.5 cm)

5. 4 teal half-square triangles
   7¼" × 7¼" (18.5 × 18.5 cm)
6. 4 gold quarter-square triangles
   7½" × 7½" (19 × 19 cm)
7. 4 white quarter-square triangles
   7½" × 7½" (19 × 19 cm)

Trim teal/white/gold units
to 6½" × 6½" (16.5 cm) square.

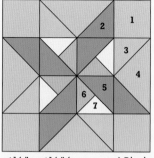

**16½" × 16½" (42 × 42 cm) Block
Make 1.**

Use:

1. 4 linen squares
   4½" × 4½" (11.15 × 11.5 cm)
2. 4 teal half-square
   triangles 4⅞" (12.25 cm)
3. 4 light blue half-square
   triangles 4⅞" (12.25 cm)
4. 4 linen quarter-square
   triangles 9¼" (23.5 × 23.5 cm)

5. 4 teal half-square triangles
   5¼" × 5¼" (13.5 × 13.5 cm)
6. 4 gold quarter-square triangles
   5½" × 5½" (14 × 14 cm)
7. 4 white quarter-square triangles
   5½" × 5½" (14 × 14 cm)

Trim teal/white/gold units to
4½" × 4½" (11.5 × 11.5 cm) square.

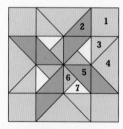

**12½" × 12½"
(31.5 × 31.5 cm) Block
Make 2.**

Use:

1. 8 linen squares
   3½" × 3½" (9 × 9 cm)
2. 8 teal half-square triangles
   3⅞" (9.75 cm)
3. 8 light blue half-square
   triangles 3⅞" (9.75 cm)
4. 8 linen quarter-square
   triangles 7¼" (18.5 cm)

5. 8 teal half-triangles
   4¼" × 4¼ (11 × 11 cm)
6. 8 gold quarter-square triangles
   4½" × 4½" (11.5 × 11.5 cm)
7. 8 white quarter-square triangles
   4½" × 4½" (11.5 × 11.5 cm)

Trim teal/white/gold units
to 3½" × 3½" (9 × 9 cm).

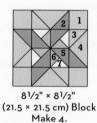

**8½" × 8½"
(21.5 × 21.5 cm) Block
Make 4.**

Use:

1. 16 linen squares
   2½" × 2½" (6.5 × 6.5 cm)
2. 16 teal half-square
   triangles 2⅞" (7.25 cm)
3. 16 light blue half-square
   triangles 2⅞" (7.25 cm)
4. 16 linen triangles
   5¼" × 5¼" (13.5 × 13.5 cm)

5. 16 teal half-triangles
   3¼" × 3¼" (8.5 × 8.5 cm)
6. 16 gold quarter-square triangles
   3½" × 3½" (9 × 9 cm)
7. 16 white quarter-square triangles
   3½" × 3½" (9 × 9 cm)

Trim teal/white/gold units
to 2½" × 2½" (6.5 × 6.5 cm) square.

Half-blocks

Make two.

1 To make the half-blocks, follow the Classic Star-and-Pinwheel block instructions, except replace the two Flying Geese units on each side of the block with half-square-triangle units.

2 Mark a diagonal line from corner to corner on the back of two linen squares 3½" × 3½" (9 × 9 cm). Pair one 3½" × 3½" (9 × 9 cm) linen square with a 3½" × 3½" (9 × 9 cm) teal square, and one 3½" × 3½" (9 × 9 cm) linen square with a 3½" × 3½" (9 × 9 cm) light blue square, right sides facing. Sew ¼" (6 mm) away from the marked diagonal on both sides. Cut along the marked diagonal and press open.

3 You will now have four half-square-triangle units—one teal/linen unit and one light blue/linen unit—for each half-block. Trim all four half-square-triangle units to 2½" × 2½" (6.5 × 6.5 cm). Trim teal/white/gold units to 2½" × 2½" (6.5 × 6.5 cm). Finish assembling the half-blocks as shown.

8½" × 4½"
(21.5 × 11.5 cm) Half-block
Make 2.

Use:

1. 2 linen quarter-square triangles 5¼" (13.5 cm)

2. 4 linen squares 2½" × 2½" (6.5 × 6.5 cm)

3. 2 teal half-square triangles 2⅞" × 2⅞" (7.25 × 7.25 cm)

4. 2 light blue half-square triangles 2⅞" × 2⅞" (7.25 × 7.25 cm)

5. 1 light blue square 3½" × 3½" (9 × 9 cm)

6. 2 linen squares 3½" × 3½" (9 × 9 cm)

7. 4 white quarter-square triangles 3½" × 3½" (9 × 9 cm)

8. 4 gold quarter-square triangles 3½" × 3½" (9 × 9 cm)

9. 4 teal half-square triangles 3¼" × 3¼" (8.5 × 8.5 cm)

10. 1 teal square 3½" × 3½" (9 × 9 cm)

Quilt Top

1 Lay out the blocks and the remaining linen pieces in sections as shown in the Sugar Snow Construction Diagram. Sew together the pieces for each section, A through G. Press.

2 Sew together the sections in the following order. Sew section B to section C and sew section D to section E. Sew section F to the bottom of section D/E. Sew Section G to the left side of section D/E/F. Sew section B/C to the top side of section D/E/F/G and section A to the top of B/C/D/E/F/G. Press.

3 Make a quilt sandwich with the backing, batting, and quilt top. Baste the layers and quilt as desired. This quilt features an allover swirl design enhanced with bubbles and a star. Trim the batting and backing to match the quilt top.

4 Join the binding strips to make a continuous length. Bind the raw edges to finish the quilt.

Sugar Snow Construction Diagram

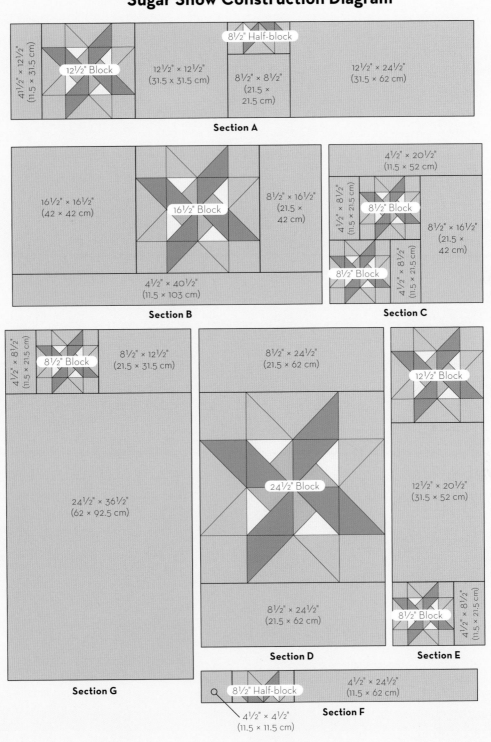

Section A

$4\frac{1}{2}" \times 12\frac{1}{2}"$
(11.5 x 31.5 cm)

12½" Block

$12\frac{1}{2}" \times 12\frac{1}{2}"$
(31.5 x 31.5 cm)

8½" Half-block

$8\frac{1}{2}" \times 8\frac{1}{2}"$
(21.5 × 21.5 cm)

$12\frac{1}{2}" \times 24\frac{1}{2}"$
(31.5 × 62 cm)

Section B

$16\frac{1}{2}" \times 16\frac{1}{2}"$
(42 × 42 cm)

16½" Block

$8\frac{1}{2}" \times 16\frac{1}{2}"$
(21.5 × 42 cm)

$4\frac{1}{2}" \times 40\frac{1}{2}"$
(11.5 × 103 cm)

Section C

$4\frac{1}{2}" \times 20\frac{1}{2}"$
(11.5 × 52 cm)

$4\frac{1}{2}" \times 8\frac{1}{2}"$
(11.5 × 21.5 cm)

8½" Block

8½" Block

$4\frac{1}{2}" \times 8\frac{1}{2}"$
(11.5 × 21.5 cm)

$8\frac{1}{2}" \times 16\frac{1}{2}"$
(21.5 × 42 cm)

Section D

$8\frac{1}{2}" \times 24\frac{1}{2}"$
(21.5 × 62 cm)

24½" Block

$8\frac{1}{2}" \times 24\frac{1}{2}"$
(21.5 × 62 cm)

Section E

12½" Block

$12\frac{1}{2}" \times 20\frac{1}{2}"$
(31.5 × 52 cm)

8½" Block

$4\frac{1}{2}" \times 8\frac{1}{2}"$
(11.5 × 21.5 cm)

Section F

8½" Half-block

$4\frac{1}{2}" \times 24\frac{1}{2}"$
(11.5 × 62 cm)

$4\frac{1}{2}" \times 4\frac{1}{2}"$
(11.5 × 11.5 cm)

Section G

$4\frac{1}{2}" \times 8\frac{1}{2}"$
(11.5 × 21.5 cm)

8½" Block

$8\frac{1}{2}" \times 12\frac{1}{2}"$
(21.5 × 31.5 cm)

$24\frac{1}{2}" \times 36\frac{1}{2}"$
(62 × 92.5 cm)

NEW COLOR APPROACHES

When we speak to fellow quilters, the conversation centers, time and time again, around color. Whether it's the difficulty of selecting the right scheme for a new project or the struggle to picture a pattern in colors of her/his own choosing, this first step in the design process can paralyze any quilter. Let's face it—color is important. Throughout this chapter, we will show you how subtle and bold color changes in blocks and backgrounds can take even the most basic quilt design and transform it to something extraordinary.

BLOCK:

Mosaic No. 19

PROJECT:

Sorbet
Mini Quilt

Designed and made by **Katie Clark Blakesley**

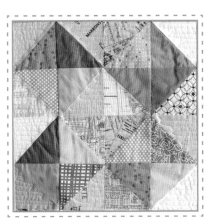

FINISHED SIZE:	TECHNIQUE USED:	SKILL LEVEL:
24" × 24" (61 × 61 cm)	Simple piecing	Beginner

DESIGN NOTE: | *Recoloring Traditional Quilt Blocks*

Often, traditional blocks such as Mosaic No. 19 have clean, simple lines. The very first design choice when planning a quilt is often how to interpret the design. In this case, the most common interpretation is to use color, pattern, and/or value to highlight the star that was usually the focus of the traditional block design. (To see the star, refer to the block illustration on page 76. The white diamond is the star center, and the surrounding white triangles are the star points.) The quilter can choose from bold or subdued colors, prints or solids, and light and dark values, or a combination of each, which will greatly change the look of the block.

With this quilt, it is possible to set aside entirely the normal block coloring, which focuses on the star. Try using a variety of solids, prints, and neutrals in a limited color palette to create a completely different look that de-emphasizes the star. Here, four Mosaic No. 19 blocks are combined. The underlying structure and orientation of the half-square triangles remains the same, only the color placement and design emphasis change. At 24" × 24" (61 × 61 cm), this quilt is sized to be decorative instead of purely functional. It can be used as a wall hanging, a pillow, a table topper, or even a doll quilt.

Katie Clark Blakesley

CLASSIC MOSAIC NO. 19 BLOCK

UNFINISHED BLOCK:
12½" × 12½" (31.5 × 31.5 cm)

Choose scraps from your stash to make this classic version for a block swap or bee. If you want to make it for a sampler quilt, see pages 146–157. This classic version is made using Flying Geese units as well as half-square triangles. To make the Sorbet Mini Quilt version, see opposite page.

Cutting

FROM WHITE FABRIC, CUT:

❑ 1 square 4¾" × 4 ½" (12 × 12 cm).

❑ 8 squares 3½" × 3½" (9 × 9 cm).

❑ 2 squares 4" × 4" (10 × 10 cm).

FROM RED FABRIC, CUT:

❑ 2 squares 3⅞" × 3⅞" (9.75 × 9.75 cm); cut diagonally to make 4 half-square triangles.

❑ 2 rectangles 3½" × 6½" (9 × 9 cm).

FROM AQUA FABRIC, CUT:

❑ 1 square 4" × 4" (10 × 10 cm).

FROM YELLOW FABRIC, CUT:

❑ 2 rectangles 3½" × 6½" (9 × 16.5 cm).

FROM GREEN SOLID OR PRINT, CUT:

❑ 1 square 4" × 4" (10 × 10 cm).

Assembling the Block

1. With a water-soluble pen or other fabric marker, mark a diagonal line on the eight white squares 3½" × 3½" (9 × 9 cm) and the two white squares 4" × 4" (10 × 10 cm).

2. To make the Flying Geese, place one white square 3½" × 3½" (9 × 9 cm) on the left side of one red rectangle 3½" × 6½" (9 × 16.5 cm), right sides

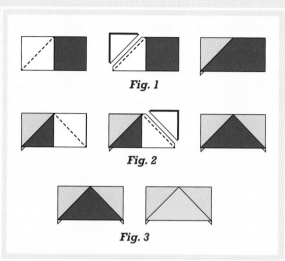

Fig. 1

Fig. 2

Fig. 3

together, with the marked diagonal line as shown *(fig. 1)*. Stitch on the line and trim the outer seam to ¼" (6 mm). Open and press the seam toward the darker fabric.

3. Place another white square 3½" × 3½" (9 × 9 cm) right side down on the right side of the red rectangle as shown *(fig. 2)*. Stitch on the line and trim the outer seam to ¼" (6 mm). Open and press the seam toward the darker fabric.

4. Repeat with the remaining marked white squares 3½" × 3½" (9 × 9 cm) and the yellow and red rectangles 3½" × 6½" (9 × 16.5 cm) to make a total of four Flying Geese *(fig. 3)*. Trim if necessary.

5. For the block corners, make four half-square-triangle units. Match one white square 4" × 4" (10 × 10 cm) with an aqua square 4" × 4" (10 × 10 cm) and the second white 4" × 4" (10 × 10 cm) square with a green square 4" × 4" (10 × 10 cm), both right sides together.

6. On each pair, sew a ¼" (6 mm) seam on both sides of the marked diagonal line. Cut each square on the drawn line. Open the resulting pairs and press the seams toward the darker fabric.

7. To square up the half-square-triangle units, align a 45-degree ruler marking with the seam and trim blocks to 3½" × 3½" (9 × 9 cm) square.

8. Place the white center square 4¾" × 4¾" (12 × 12 cm) on-point and sew two red half-square triangles opposite each other *(fig. 4).* (Make sure triangle corners hang over the square edges ¼" (6 mm) on each side.) Press. Sew the remaining two red half-square triangles opposite each other *(fig. 5)* and press well.

9. Lay out the block as shown in *fig. 6*. Pin and sew one white-and-yellow Flying Geese unit to each side of the center square. Press.

10. Sew the corner half-square-triangle units on both ends of remaining two white-and-red Flying Geese, alternating colors. Press.

11. Sew the top and bottom rows to the center row. Press.

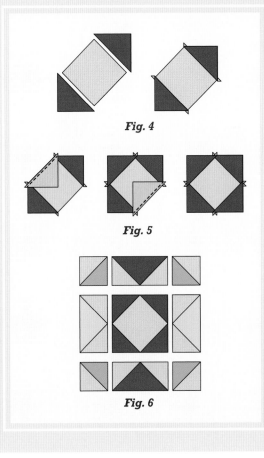

Fig. 4

Fig. 5

Fig. 6

MAKE THE SORBET MINI QUILT

Materials
All fabric amounts are for 45" (114.5 cm) wide fabric.

Note: *You can use a fat quarter (18" × 22") (45.5 × 56 cm) of a print or solid in each color or scraps of coordinating prints and solids in each color from your stash.*

- 1 fat quarter each of neutral print and solid
- 1 fat quarter of text print
- 1 fat quarter of teal print or solid
- 1 fat quarter of orange print or solid
- 1 fat quarter of pink print or solid
- 1 fat quarter of plum print or solid
- 1 fat quarter of red-orange print or solid
- ⅞ yd (80 cm) backing fabric
- 28" × 28" (71 × 71 cm) low-loft cotton batting
- ¼ yd (23 cm) binding fabric

Tools
- Water-soluble pen or other fabric marker

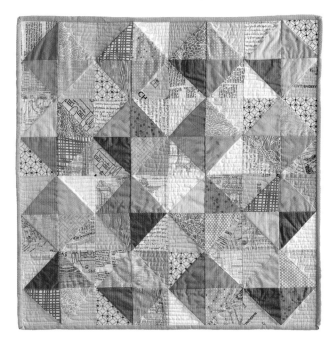

Cutting

FROM NEUTRAL PRINT FABRIC, CUT:

☐ 8 squares 4" × 4" (10 × 10 cm).

FROM NEUTRAL SOLID FABRIC, CUT:

☐ 12 squares 4" × 4" (10 × 10 cm).

FROM TEXT PRINT FABRIC, CUT:

☐ 12 squares 4" × 4" (10 × 10 cm).

FROM TEAL SOLID OR PRINT FABRIC, CUT:

☐ 8 squares 4" × 4" (10 × 10 cm).

FROM ORANGE SOLID OR PRINT FABRIC, CUT:

☐ 6 squares 4" × 4" (10 × 10 cm).

FROM PINK SOLID OR PRINT FABRIC, CUT:

☐ 6 squares 4" × 4" (10 × 10 cm).

FROM PLUM SOLID OR PRINT FABRIC, CUT:

☐ 6 squares 4" × 4" (10 × 10 cm).

FROM RED-ORANGE SOLID OR PRINT FABRIC, CUT:

☐ 6 squares 4" × 4" (10 × 10 cm).

FROM BINDING FABRIC, CUT:

☐ 3 strips 2½" (6.5 cm) × width of fabric.

Mosaic No. 19 Blocks

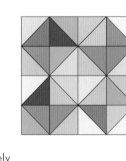

UNFINISHED BLOCK:
12½" × 12½" (31.5 × 31.5 cm)

Unlike the Classic Mosaic No. 19 block, which uses half-square triangles and Flying Geese, the Sorbet Mini Quilt is made exclusively of half-square-triangle units. Although the finished quilt looks different than the star in the Mosaic No. 19 block, all of the half-square-triangle pairs are oriented the same way.

1 With a water-soluble pen or other fabric marker, mark a diagonal line on all thirty-two of the neutral solid, neutral print, and text print fabric squares.

2 Pair a neutral solid, print, or text square with each of the colored squares. Use a variety of combinations to create the most interest. Match up the pairs right sides together and sew a ¼" (6 mm) seam on both sides of the marked diagonal line.

3 Cut each square on the drawn line to make two half-square-triangle units. Open and press the seams toward the darker fabric.

4 To square up the half-square-triangle units, align a 45-degree ruler marking with the seam and trim blocks to 3½" × 3½" (9 × 9 cm) square. Trim all sixty-four half-square-triangle units as necessary.

Quilt Top

1 Refer to the Sorbet Mini Quilt Construction Diagram to lay out the sixty-four half-square-triangle units in eight rows of eight blocks each. Be sure to pay attention to which way the neutral and color halves are oriented.

2 Sew the half-square-triangle units together in horizontal rows. Press each individual block. Press the seams for odd-numbered rows (1, 3, 5, and 7) to the left and seams for even-numbered rows (2, 4, 6, and 8) to the right.

3 Sew together the rows in order, taking care to match and nest seams.

4 Make a quilt sandwich with the backing, batting, and quilt top. Baste the layers and quilt as desired. Trim the batting and backing to match the quilt top.

5 Join the binding strips to make a continuous length. Bind the raw edges to finish the quilt.

6 If you want to hang it on the wall, use your favorite method to add a hanging sleeve on the back.

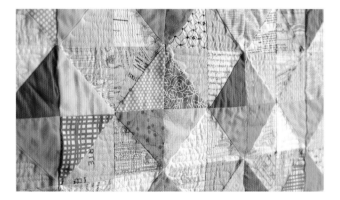

Sorbet Mini Quilt Construction Diagram

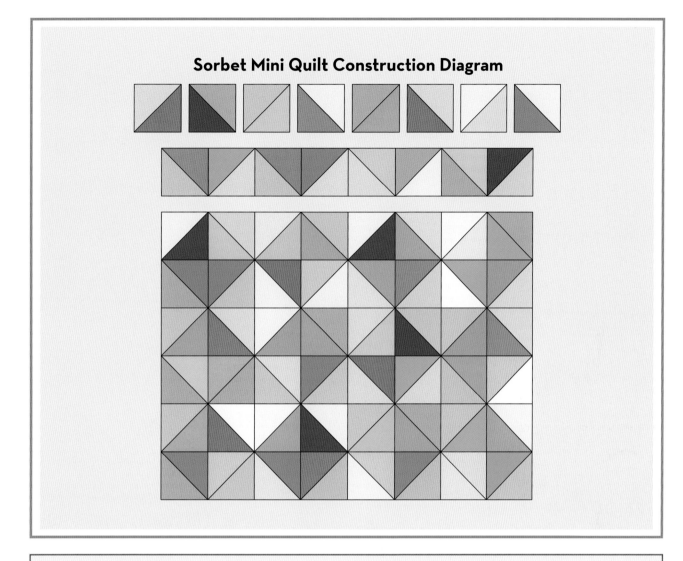

MINI HISTORY LESSON: *Doll Quilts*

Often, quilts that are smaller than 24" × 24" (61 × 61 cm) are called "mini quilts" or "doll quilts." In the nineteenth and early twentieth centuries, mothers used doll quilts to teach their daughters to sew. This practice was called "fireside training." Girls as young as three or four learned to stitch simple blocks, such as a Nine Patch, even before they learned to read. As recorded in the Quilt Discovery Experience, Homestead National Monument of America, Beatrice, Nebraska, nineteenth-century pioneer Edith White recalled, "Before I was five years old, I had pieced one side of a quilt, sitting at my mother's knee half an hour a day." (www.nps .gov/home/planyourvisit/upload/quilt-brochure-re-worked-pg-1.pdf).

Today, doll quilts are quite popular. Many online international swaps feature quilts sized between 12" × 12" (30.5 × 30.5 cm) and 24" × 24" (61 × 61 cm). By working with smaller blocks, quiltmakers can try new patterns, practice new techniques, and improve their skills, much as their younger counterparts did in the past.

BLOCK:

Diamond Panes

PROJECT:

Rosy Windows Quilt

Designed and made by **Faith Jones**

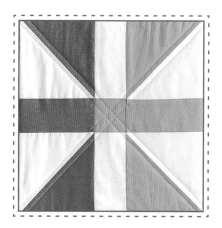

FINISHED SIZE:	**TECHNIQUE USED:**	**SKILL LEVEL:**
48" × 60" (122 × 152.5 cm)	Simple piecing	Beginner

DESIGN NOTE:	*Updating Historical Quilt Color Schemes*

This quilt is a modern take on the traditional red-and-white color scheme that was popular in the nineteenth century. To give this color scheme a fresh new look, I used an additional shade of red in one column of quilt blocks and added small "pops" of other colors in the block centers.

Using various shades of one color—either distinctly in one section of the quilt as shown here or scattered throughout the entire quilt top—gives the project an unexpected and exciting feel. Consider applying this technique not only to freshen up traditional red-and-white designs, but also to enliven blue-and-white or black-and-white quilts.

CLASSIC DIAMOND PANES BLOCK

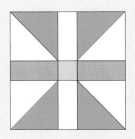

UNFINISHED BLOCK: 12½" × 12½" (31.5 × 31. 5 cm)

Choose scraps from your stash to make this classic version for a block swap or bee. If you want to make it for a sampler quilt, see pages 146–157. To make the Rosy Windows Quilt version, see opposite page.

Cutting

FROM AQUA FABRIC, CUT:

❑ 2 squares 6⅜" × 6⅜" (16.3 × 16.3 cm); cut in half diagonally to make 4 half-square triangles.

FROM ORANGE FABRIC, CUT:

❑ 2 rectangles 2½" × 5½" (6.5 × 14 cm).

FROM WHITE FABRIC, CUT:

❑ 2 squares 6⅜" × 6⅜" (16.3 × 16.3 cm); cut in half diagonally to make 4 half-square triangles.

❑ 2 rectangles 2½" × 5½" (6.5 × 14 cm).

FROM YELLOW FABRIC, CUT:

❑ 1 square 2½" × 2½" (6.5 × 6.5 cm).

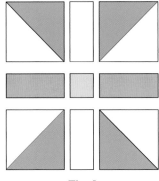

Fig. 1

Assembling the Block

1. Match the four aqua half-square triangles to the four white half-square triangles. Sew each pair together along the diagonal edges. Open and press. Trim each resulting square to 5½" × 5½" (14 × 14 cm).

2. Lay out the half-square triangles and the remaining cut pieces as shown *(fig. 1)*.

3. Sew together the pieces in each row. Press.

4. Sew the rows together. Press.

MAKE THE ROSY WINDOWS QUILT

Materials

All fabric amounts are for 45" (114.5 cm) wide fabric.

- 1 yd (91.5 cm) dark red fabric
- 1 yd (91.5 cm) light red fabric
- ⅛ yd (11.5 cm) orange fabric
- ⅛ yd (11.5 cm) yellow fabric
- ⅛ yd 11.5 cm) blue fabric
- ⅛ yd (11.5 cm) green fabric
- 1¾ yd (1.6 m) white fabric
- 3⅛ yd (2.86 m) backing fabric
- 56" × 68" (142 × 172.7 cm) low-loft cotton batting
- ½ yd (45.5 cm) binding fabric

Cutting

FROM DARK RED FABRIC, CUT:

❏ 20 squares 6⅜" × 6⅜" (16.3 × 16.3 cm); cut in half diagonally to make 40 half-square triangles.

❏ 20 rectangles 2½" × 5½" (6.5 × 14 cm).

FROM LIGHT RED FABRIC, CUT:

❏ 20 squares 6⅜" × 6⅜" (16.3 × 16.3 cm); cut in half diagonally to make 40 half-square triangles.

❏ 20 strips 2½" × 5½" (6.5 × 14 cm).

FROM ORANGE FABRIC, CUT:

❏ 5 squares 2½" × 2½" (6.5 × 6.5 cm).

FROM YELLOW FABRIC, CUT:

❏ 5 squares 2½" × 2½" (6.5 × 6.5 cm).

FROM BLUE FABRIC, CUT:

❏ 5 squares 2½" × 2½" (6.5 × 6.5 cm).

FROM GREEN FABRIC, CUT:

❏ 5 squares 2½" × 2½" (6.5 × 6.5 cm).

FROM WHITE FABRIC, CUT:

❏ 40 squares 6⅜" × 6⅜" (16.3 × 16.3 cm); cut in half diagonally to make 80 half-square triangles.

❏ 40 strips 2½" × 5½" (6.5 × 14 cm).

FROM BINDING FABRIC, CUT:

❏ 6 strips 2½" (6.5 cm) × width of fabric.

Diamond Pane Blocks

UNFINISHED BLOCK:
12½" × 12½" (31.5 × 31.5 cm)

Follow the Classic Diamond Panes block instructions to make twenty blocks.

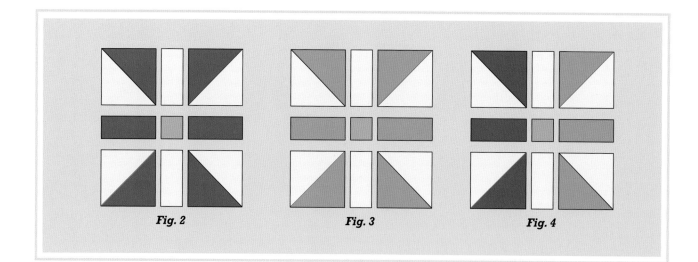

Fig. 2   Fig. 3   Fig. 4

1 For the first five blocks, use all dark red fabric (*fig. 2*). For the block center squares 2½" × 2½" (6.5 × 6.5 cm), make two blocks with green centers, one with a yellow center, one with an orange center, and one with a blue center.

2 For the second five blocks, use all light red fabric (*fig. 3*). For the block center squares 2½" × 2½" (6.5 × 6.5 cm), make two blocks with blue centers, one with a yellow center, one with an orange center, and one with a green center.

3 For the remaining ten blocks, use dark red fabric on the left side of the block and light red fabric on the right side (*fig. 4*). For the block center squares 2½" × 2½" (6.5 × 6.5 cm), make three blocks with yellow centers, three blocks with orange centers, two blocks with blue centers, and two blocks with green centers.

Quilt Top

1 Refer to the Rosy Windows Construction Diagram to lay out the blocks in four columns of five blocks each, alternating the orientation of the blocks in each column as shown. Note the color placement. From left to right: Column 1 has dark red/light red blocks; column 2 has light red blocks; column 3 has light red/dark red blocks; and column 4 has dark red blocks.

2 Sew together the blocks. Press the seams open to reduce bulk. Sew together the rows. Press.

MINI HISTORY LESSON: *Red-and-White Quilts*

Many of the vintage red-and-white quilts you come across today were made in the nineteenth century using "Turkey red" cotton, which was made with a special dye process and did not bleed or fade. This colorfast fabric was available years before much less expensive red synthetic dyes entered the market. The results were bold quilts with colors that are still vibrant more than one hundred years later. Unfortunately, quilts made using the synthetic red dyes faded to brown or peach and tended to bleed. Until the synthetic reds were improved to prevent these issues, quilters who were able to pay more money for their fabrics still used Turkey red cotton.

3 Make a quilt sandwich with the backing, batting, and quilt top. Baste the layers and quilt as desired. I did very simple straight-line quilting. Trim the batting and backing to match the quilt top.

4 Join the binding strips to make a continuous length. Bind the raw edges to finish the quilt.

Rosy Windows Construction Diagram

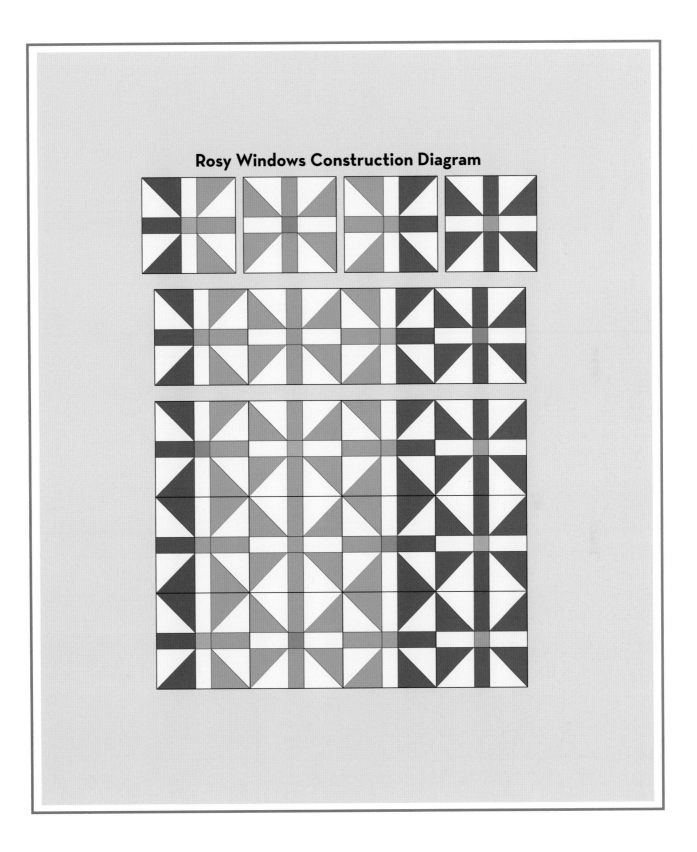

BLOCK:
Wheel of Fortune

PROJECT:
Spin It Again Quilt

Designed and made by **Lee Heinrich**

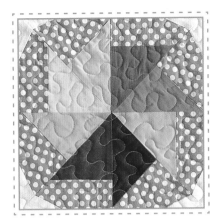

FINISHED SIZE:	TECHNIQUE USED:	SKILL LEVEL:
48" × 60" (122 × 152.5 cm)	Foundation piecing	Intermediate

DESIGN NOTE: | *Try Something Unexpected*

I had originally planned to make this as a typical scrap quilt, but eventually I decided that wasn't a very unique take on this design. I tried a number of different strategies to freshen it up, but none seemed to work with this particular block. Finally, I started thinking less about design and more about just doing something unexpected—and that turned out to be as simple as using a print for the block background instead of a solid and placing the solids where I had previously planned to use scraps of prints.

So if you're stumped for design inspiration, take a hard look at the variables you would not normally think about changing, such as placement of solids versus prints. This is such a simple modification, but one that makes this quilt unique and memorable. It's unexpected changes such as these that have made modern quilting what it is.

CLASSIC WHEEL OF FORTUNE BLOCK

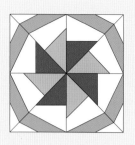

UNFINISHED BLOCK:
12½" × 12½" (31.5 × 31.5 cm)

Choose scraps from your stash to make this classic version for a block swap or bee. If you want to make it for a sampler quilt, see pages 146–157. To make the Spin It Again Quilt version, see opposite page. Wheel of Fortune templates A and B are on the CD included with this book.

Cutting

FROM WHITE FABRIC, CUT:

❐ 8 rectangles 3½" × 5½" (9 × 14 cm) (template pieces A2 and B3).

❐ 8 rectangles 2½" × 5" (6.5 × 12.5 cm) (template pieces A4 and B1).

FROM AQUA FABRIC, CUT:

❐ 8 strips 2½" × 6" (6.5 × 15 cm) (template pieces A3 and B2).

FROM RED FABRIC, CUT:

❐ 2 squares 5" × 5" (12.5 × 12.5 cm); cut in half diagonally to make 4 half-square triangles (template piece A1).

FROM ORANGE FABRIC, CUT:

❐ 2 squares 5" × 5" (12.5 × 12.5 cm); cut in half diagonally to make 4 half-square triangles (template piece B4).

Assembling the Block

1. Print and cut out four copies of *each* Wheel of Fortune Template at 100 percent.

2. Using the technique described in Guide to Foundation Piecing (page 13), piece eight Wheel of Fortune templates. Use the cutting instructions above to identify which fabric pieces correspond to each number.

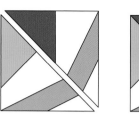

Fig.1

Fig.2

Tip

Template B numbers go in the reverse direction of template A. This means that the seams will be pressed in opposite directions, allowing for easier seam alignment when the two sections are joined.

3. Pin and sew each A section to a B section along the diagonal edge *(fig. 1)*.

4. Sew these four units together to complete the block *(fig. 2)*.

MAKE THE SPIN IT AGAIN QUILT

Materials

All fabric amounts are for 45" (114.5 cm) wide fabric.

- 3¾ yd (3.45 m) gray dot print fabric
- 1¾ yd (1.6 m) white solid fabric
- ¼ yd (23 cm) each of 8 solid colors
- 3¼ yd (2.97 m) backing fabric
- 56" × 68" (142 × 172.7 cm) low-loft cotton batting
- ½ yd (45.5 cm) binding fabric

Tools

- Wheel of Fortune templates A and B*
- Foundation-piecing paper

* *You will need to print eighty copies of each Wheel of Fortune Template at 100 percent.*

Cutting

FROM WHITE SOLID FABRIC, CUT:

❐ 160 strips 2½" × 6" (6.5 × 15 cm) (template pieces A3 and B2).

FROM GRAY DOT PRINT FABRIC, CUT:

❐ 160 rectangles 3½" × 5½" (9 × 14 cm) (template pieces A2 and B3).

❐ 160 rectangles 2½" × 5" (6.5 × 12.5 cm) (template pieces A4 and B1).

FROM EACH SOLID FABRIC, CUT:

❐ 10 squares 5" × 5" (12.5 × 12.5 cm); cut in half diagonally to make 160 half-square triangles (template pieces A1 and B4).

FROM BINDING FABRIC, CUT:

❐ 6 strips 2½" (6.5 cm) × width of fabric.

Wheel of Fortune Blocks

UNFINISHED BLOCK:
12½" × 12½" (31.5 × 31.5 cm)

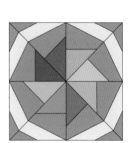

Follow the Classic Wheel of Fortune block instructions to make twenty Wheel of Fortune blocks. Use the cutting instructions to identify which fabric pieces correspond to each template number and note color placement within the block.

Quilt Top

1 Lay out the quilt top in five rows of four blocks each as shown in the Spin It Again Construction Diagram.

2 Sew together the blocks in each row. Press the seams for each row in alternating directions. Sew the rows together to complete the quilt top. Press.

3 Make a quilt sandwich with the backing, batting, and quilt top. Baste the layers and quilt as desired. This quilt features an allover meandering pattern. Trim the batting and backing to match the quilt top.

4 Join the binding strips to make a continuous length. Bind the raw edges to finish the quilt.

MINI HISTORY LESSON: *Scrap Quilts*

Scrap quilts often bring to mind the image of a resourceful pioneer woman cutting up worn clothing to create bedcovers for her family. But the truth may be that scrap quilting didn't become as commonplace as we think until the Great Depression, when hard-pressed quiltmakers were forced to use every bit of fabric they had on hand. Along with feed sacks, women also used bits of old clothing, worn-out bed linens, and anything else they could get their hands on. Often quilters made "britches quilts" from men's old denim work clothes or wool clothing.

When scraps were used, it was often in the form of small units for Nine Patch blocks, small hexagons (as in a Grandmother's Flower Garden quilt), half-square triangles, or Log Cabin blocks. Log Cabin and half-square-triangle scrap quilts were often made as value studies, with lighter scraps contrasting with the darker pieces. Today, these are still popular ways for quilters to use their scraps.

Spin It Again Construction Diagram

BLOCK:
Tilted Star

PROJECT:
Cosmos Baby Quilt

*Designed and made by **Faith Jones***

FINISHED SIZE:	TECHNIQUES USED:	SKILL LEVEL:
36" × 48" (91.5 × 122 cm)	Foundation piecing, partial seams	Intermediate

---

DESIGN NOTE: *Background Color*

Add dimension and interest to any quilt by using slightly different shades of a single neutral color as the background for each block. This technique helps define the space of individual blocks and adds some depth and texture to the background. The resulting quilt is pleasing to the eye because, although the background fabrics vary, they are all based on a common color element such as tan or gray.

Of course, you could also use a different color for the block centers, which would add yet another variation. Although the Tilted Star block design first appeared seventy years ago, it has the same styling as many improvisational, or "wonky," star blocks used in modern quilts today. The combination of this quilt's color scheme and the wonky stars makes this a fun and different baby quilt design that could also be used as a wall hanging.

CLASSIC TILTED STAR BLOCK

UNFINISHED BLOCK: 12½" × 12½" (31.5 × 31.5 cm)

Choose scraps from your stash to make this classic version for a block swap or bee. If you want to make it for a sampler quilt, see pages 146–157. To make the Cosmos Baby Quilt version, see opposite page. The Tilted Star Template is on the CD included with this book.

Cutting

FROM CREAM FABRIC, CUT:

❑ 1 square 5⅞" × 5⅞" (14.75 × 14.75 cm).

FROM A VARIETY OF SCRAPPY PRINT FABRICS, CUT:

❑ 4 rectangles 4" × 7" (10 × 18 cm) (template piece 1).

❑ 2 squares 5" × 5" (12.5 × 12.5 cm); cut in half diagonally to make 4 half-square triangles (template piece 4).

FROM WHITE BACKGROUND FABRIC, CUT:

❑ 4 rectangles 4" × 7" (10 × 18 cm) (template piece 2).

❑ 4 rectangles 5" × 7" (12. 5 × 18 cm) (template piece 3).

Assembling the Block

1. Print and cut out four copies of the Tilted Star Template at 100 percent.

2. Using the technique described in Guide to Foundation Piecing (page 13), piece four templates. Use the cutting instructions to identify which fabric pieces correspond to each template number.

3. Use the technique described in Guide to Partial Seams (page 14) to sew the four foundation-pieced units to the 5⅞" × 5⅞" (14.75 × 14.75 cm) star center square. Start with the top star points and work your way clockwise around the block *(fig. 1)*.

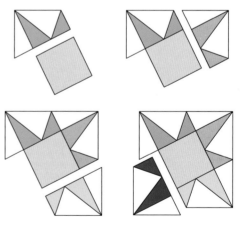

Fig. 1

MAKE THE COSMOS BABY QUILT

Materials

All fabric amounts are for 45" (114.5 cm) wide fabric.

- ³⁄₈ yd (34.5 cm) white fabric
- 1¹⁄₂ yd (137 cm) *total* of various scrappy print fabrics
- ²⁄₃ yd (61 cm) light tan fabric
- ²⁄₃ yd (61 cm) medium-light tan fabric
- ²⁄₃ yd (61 cm) medium-dark tan fabric
- 1 yd (91.5 cm) dark tan fabric
- 2¹⁄₂ yd (2.3 m) backing fabric
- 44" × 56" (114.5 × 142 cm) low-loft cotton batting
- ¹⁄₂ yd (45.5 cm) binding fabric

Tools

- Tilted Star Template*
- Foundation-piecing paper

* You will need to print fifty-two copies of the Tilted Star Template at 100 percent.

Cutting

FROM WHITE FABRIC, CUT:

❒ 13 squares 5⁷⁄₈" × 5⁷⁄₈" (14.75 × 14.75 cm).

FROM SCRAPPY PRINT FABRICS, CUT:

❒ 52 rectangles 4" × 7" (10 × 18 cm) (template piece 1).

❒ 26 squares 5" × 5" (12.5 × 12.5 cm); cut in half diagonally to make 52 half-square triangles (template piece 4).

FROM LIGHT TAN FABRIC, CUT:

❒ 12 rectangles 4" × 7" (10 × 18 cm) (template piece 2).

❒ 12 rectangles 5" × 7" (12.5 × 18 cm) (template piece 3).

FROM MEDIUM-LIGHT TAN FABRIC, CUT:

❒ 12 rectangles 4" × 7" (10 × 18 cm) (template piece 2).

❒ 12 rectangles 5" × 7" (12.5 × 18 cm) (template piece 3).

FROM MEDIUM-DARK TAN FABRIC, CUT:

❒ 12 rectangles 4" × 7" (10 × 18 cm) (template piece 2).

❒ 12 rectangles 5" × 7" (12.5 × 18 cm) (template piece 3).

FROM DARK TAN FABRIC, CUT:

❒ 16 rectangles 4" × 7" (10 × 18 cm) (template piece 2).

❒ 16 rectangles 5" × 7" (12.5 × 18 cm) (template piece 3).

FROM BINDING FABRIC, CUT:

❒ 5 strips 2¹⁄₂" (6.5 cm) × width of fabric.

Tilted Star Blocks

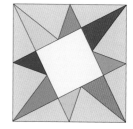

UNFINISHED BLOCK:
12¹⁄₂" × 12¹⁄₂" (31.5 × 31.5 cm)

Follow the Classic Tilted Star block instructions to make thirteen blocks. Use the cutting instructions to identify which fabric pieces correspond to each template number.

Make three blocks *each* using the light tan background fabric, the medium-light tan background fabric, and the medium-dark tan background fabric. Make four blocks using the dark tan background fabric.

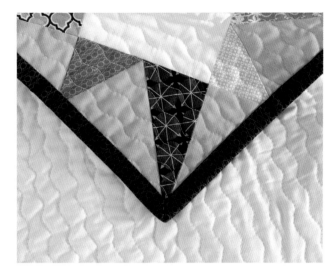

Quilt Top

1 Lay out the blocks in columns, in a staggered configuration as shown in *fig. 2*.

2 Take the top and bottom blocks from the middle column and trim each to 6½" × 12½" (16.5 × 31.5 cm) *(fig. 3)*. This will allow for the extra seam allowance needed due to the staggering of the blocks. Discard the smaller portions.

3 Refer to the Cosmos Construction Diagram to sew together the quilt top. Sew the blocks into columns. Sew together the columns, taking care to align the star points at the corners. Press seams open to reduce bulk.

4 Make a quilt sandwich with the backing, batting, and quilt top. Baste the layers and quilt as desired. I stitched parallel, wavy lines over the entire quilt top to give it an interesting texture. Trim the batting and backing to match the quilt top.

5 Join the binding strips to make a continuous length. Bind the raw edges to finish the quilt.

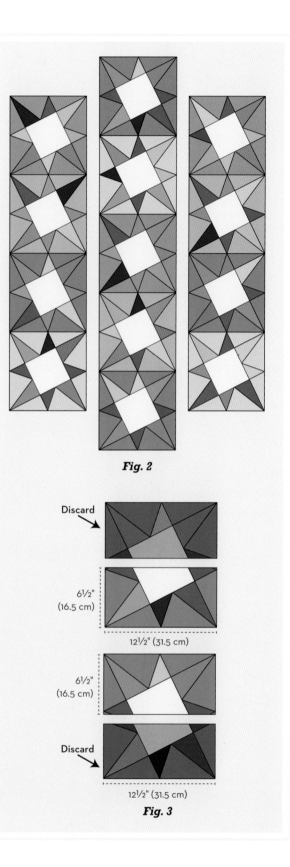

Fig. 2

Discard

6½" (16.5 cm)

12½" (31.5 cm)

6½" (16.5 cm)

Discard

12½" (31.5 cm)

Fig. 3

Cosmos Construction Diagram

MINI HISTORY LESSON:
Sawtooth Star Block

The Tilted Star block is a variation of the Sawtooth Star, one of the most traditional and popular star quilt blocks, which dates back more than two hundred years. The Sawtooth Star is a simple Nine Patch quilt block made from five squares and four Flying Geese elements. The classic simplicity of this pattern not only makes it a great block for those learning to quilt, but its design can also be easily altered a bit to create an entirely fresh-looking square.

The Tilted Star version used in this quilt was an unnamed block that—according to Barbara Brackman in *Encyclopedia of Pieced Quilt Patterns*—first appeared in *McCall's Book of Needlework*, Winter 1942/1943. Even though it is seventy years old, this pattern has a very modern look.

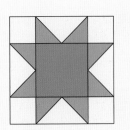

Sawtooth Star

BLOCK:
Cross and Crown

PROJECT:
Seaside Quilt

*Designed and made by **Katie Clark Blakesley***
*Quilted by **Cindy Luby***

FINISHED SIZE:	**TECHNIQUE USED:**	**SKILL LEVEL:**
60" × 72" (152.5 × 182.9 cm)	Foundation piecing	Intermediate

DESIGN NOTE: | *Using the Color Wheel*

Most often, the first thing you see when you look at a quilt is color. Subtle changes in color can make a big impact on the look of a finished quilt.

Concepts of color mixing and the visual effect of different color combinations fall under the heading of color theory, which is essentially based on the color wheel.

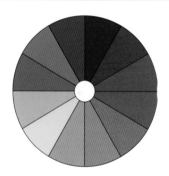

The Seaside quilt uses a harmonizing color scheme, which is made primarily from two colors next to each other on the color wheel—blue-green and blue. This quilt cheats a little bit and throws in "pops" of yellow-green, or chartreuse, for good measure. Imagine how different this quilt would look made with another color scheme—for example, a red and green Christmas quilt using complementary colors (colors that are across from each other in the color wheel). Or picture it made with green in place of yellow-green, in an analogous color scheme (three colors that are next to each other on the color wheel). For a very user-friendly discussion of color, see Jeni Baker's series, "The Art of Choosing," at www.incolororder.com.

Katie Clark Blakesley

CLASSIC CROSS AND CROWN BLOCK

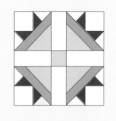

UNFINISHED BLOCK:

12½" × 12½" (31.5 × 31.5 cm)

Choose scraps from your stash to make this classic version for a block swap or bee. If you want to make it for a sampler quilt, see pages 146–157. To make the Seaside Quilt version, see opposite page. The Cross and Crown Template is on the CD included with this book.

Cutting

FROM WHITE FABRIC, CUT:

- ❑ 4 squares 3½" × 3½" (9 × 9 cm) (template piece 1).

- ❑ 4 squares 3" × 3" (7.5 × 7.5 cm); cut in half diagonally to make 8 half-square triangles (template pieces 4 and 5).

- ❑ 4 rectangles 2½" × 5½" (6.5 × 14 cm).

FROM RED FABRIC, CUT:

- ❑ 4 squares 3" × 3" (7.5 × 7.5 cm); cut in half diagonally to make 8 half-square triangles (template pieces 2 and 3).

FROM GREEN FABRIC, CUT:

- ❑ 4 strips 2" × 9" (5 × 23 cm) (template piece 6).

FROM YELLOW FABRIC, CUT:

- ❑ 2 squares 5½" × 5½" (14 × 14 cm); cut in half diagonally to make 4 half-square triangles (template piece 7).

- ❑ 1 square 2½" × 2½" (6.5 × 6.5 cm).

Fig. 1

Assembling the Block

1. Print and cut out four copies of the Cross and Crown Template at 100 percent.

2. Using the technique described in Guide to Foundation Piecing (page 13), piece four templates. Use the cutting instructions above to identify which fabric pieces correspond to each template number.

3. Lay out the pieced units with the four white rectangles 2½" × 5½" (6.5 × 14 cm) and the yellow center square 2½" × 2½" (6.5 × 6.5 cm), as shown in *fig. 1.*

4. Sew together the two pieced units and one white rectangle to make the top row. Repeat to make the bottom row. Press.

5. Sew one white rectangle to each side of the chartreuse center square to make the middle row. Press.

6. Sew the top and bottom rows to the middle row, aligning seams. Press.

MAKE THE SEASIDE QUILT

Note: *This quilt design is very versatile. Simply changing the size of the surrounding turquoise area, the color of the solid, or the number of blocks will result in a quilt of a different look and feel.*

Materials

All fabric amounts are for 45" (114.5 cm) wide fabric.

- 1¼ yd (114.5 cm) white solid fabric
- ½ yd (45.5 cm) turquoise print fabric, or equivalent scraps of turquoise print fabrics
- ½ yd (45.5 cm) blue print fabric, or equivalent scraps of blue print fabrics
- ⅔ yd (61 cm) chartreuse solid fabric, or equivalent scraps of chartreuse solid and print fabrics
- 3½ yd (3.2 m) turquoise solid fabric
- 4½ yd (4.2 m) backing fabric
- 68" × 80" (172.7 × 203.2 cm) low-loft cotton batting
- ¾ yd (68.5 cm) binding fabric

Tools

- Cross and Crown Template *
- Foundation-piecing paper

* You will need to print forty copies of the Cross and Crown Template at 100 percent.

Cutting

FROM WHITE FABRIC, CUT:

- ❑ 40 squares 3½" × 3½" (9 × 9 cm) (template piece 1).

- ❑ 40 squares 3" × 3" (7.5 × 7.5 cm); cut in half diagonally to make 80 half-square triangles (template pieces 4 and 5).

- ❑ 40 rectangles 2½" × 5½" (6.5 × 14 cm).

FROM TURQUOISE PRINT FABRIC, CUT:

- ❑ 40 squares 3" × 3" (7.5 × 7.5 cm); cut in half diagonally to make 80 half-square triangles (template pieces 2 and 3).

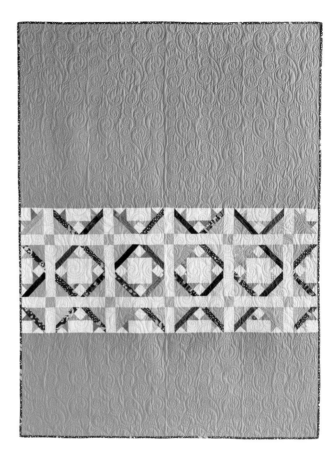

FROM BLUE PRINT FABRIC, CUT:

- ❑ 40 strips 2" × 9" (5 × 23 cm) (template piece 6).

FROM CHARTREUSE SOLID FABRIC, CUT:

- ❑ 20 squares 5½" × 5½" (14 × 14 cm); cut in half diagonally to make 40 half-square triangles (template piece 7).

- ❑ 10 squares 2½" × 2½" (6.5 × 6.5 cm).

FROM TURQUOISE SOLID FABRIC, CUT:

- ❑ 1 rectangle 18½" × 60½" (47 × 153.5 cm) (cut lengthwise).

- ❑ 1 rectangle 30½" × 60½" (77.5 × 153.5 cm) (cut lengthwise).

FROM BINDING FABRIC, CUT:

- ❑ 8 strips 2½" (6.5 cm) × width of fabric.

Cross and Crown Block

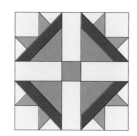

UNFINISHED BLOCK:

12½" × 12½" (31.5 × 31.5 cm)

Follow the Classic Cross and Crown block instructions to make ten blocks. Use the cutting instructions to identify which fabric pieces correspond to each template number.

Quilt Top

1 Lay out the ten blocks in two rows of five blocks each, as shown in the Cross and Crown Construction Diagram.

2 Sew together the blocks in the top row, aligning seams. Press. Repeat to make the bottom row.

3 Pin and sew the 18½" × 60½" (47 × 153.5 cm) strip of turquoise solid fabric to the bottom of the block section; press.

4 Pin and sew the 30½" × 60½" (77.5 × 153.5 cm) rectangle of turquoise solid fabric to the top of the block section; press.

5 Make a quilt sandwich with the backing, batting, and quilt top. Baste the layers and quilt as desired. Trim the batting and backing to match the quilt top.

6 Join the binding strips to make a continuous length. Bind the raw edges to finish the quilt.

MINI HISTORY LESSON:
The Nancy Page Quilt Club

The block in this quilt, commonly known as Cross and Crown and published as block No. 151 by the Ladies Art Company in 1897, was also published by "Nancy Page" under the name Bouquet's Wreath.

Nancy Page was the pen name of Florence La Ganke, who started a weekly syndicated column in the late 1920s. In 1929, taking advantage of the increasing popularity of quilting throughout the United States, she started the Nancy Page Quilt Club. In the column, "Nancy" invited fictional friends to join her in a weekly quilting club and published their "experiences."

Her column provided more than six hundred patterns to readers during the fifteen or so years it was published. These included patterns to make twenty-one different sampler-style quilts, the majority of which were appliqué based.

Seaside Construction Diagram

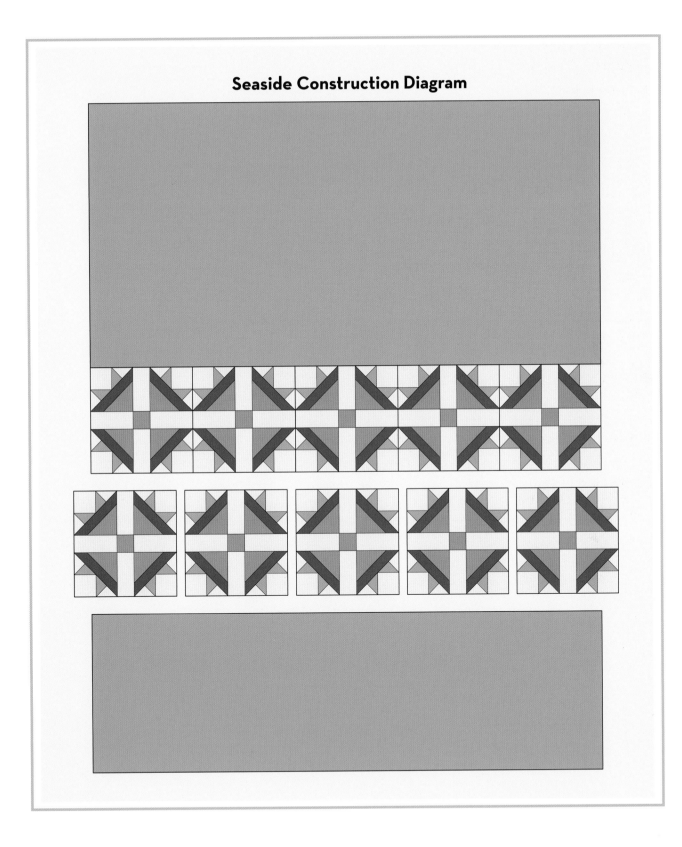

BLOCK:

Exploding Star

PROJECT:

Star Bright Quilt

*Designed and made by **Faith Jones***

FINISHED SIZE:	TECHNIQUE USED:	SKILL LEVEL:
60" × 72" (152.5 × 182.9 cm)	Foundation piecing	Advanced

DESIGN NOTE:	*Warm and Cool Colors*

Selecting fabrics for a quilt pattern can be the most difficult and intimidating part of the process. Following a few color rules can make this challenge a bit easier and also create a quilt that is pleasing to the eye. Consider making some blocks using all warm colors—reds, pinks, oranges, and yellows—and some blocks using all cool colors—greens, blues, and purples. Some of my favorite designs limit the number of colors in the quilt to two or three, but use various shades of each. For example, if you are using red, orange, and yellow only, select five different shades of fabric in each color family. The quilt will suddenly have a dynamic jeweled feel to it.

Perhaps you can incorporate a common element into each block. This might be a text fabric or a fabric that reads as a neutral, such as tan or gray. These fabrics are great unifiers when used consistently throughout your quilt. It's not necessary to use them in each block, but scattering them throughout creates added interest. Taking time to follow through with these choices as you make your quilt will lead to a cohesive design.

CLASSIC EXPLODING STAR BLOCK

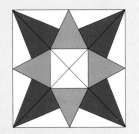

UNFINISHED BLOCK:
12½" × 12½" (31.5 × 31.5 cm)

Choose scraps from your stash to make this classic version for a block swap or bee. The star center and block background are light neutral, the small star points are a single color, and the large star points are light and dark values of another color. If you want to make it for a sampler quilt, see pages 146–157. To make the Star Bright Quilt version, see opposite page. Exploding Star templates A and B are on the CD included with this book.

Cutting

FROM WHITE FABRIC, CUT:

☐ 8 rectangles 3½" × 7" (9 × 18 cm) (template pieces A2 and B2).

☐ 2 squares 5" × 5" (12.5 × 12.5 cm); cut in half diagonally to make 4 half-square triangles (template piece A4).

FROM PINK AND RED FABRICS, CUT:

☐ 8 rectangles 3½" × 7" (9 × 18 cm) (template pieces A1 and B1).

FROM ORANGE FABRIC, CUT:

☐ 4 rectangles 5" × 6" (12.5 × 15 cm) (template piece A3).

Assembling the Block

1. Print and cut out four copies of *each* Exploding Star Template at 100 percent.

2. Using the technique described in Guide to Foundation Piecing (page 13), piece eight templates, noting the color positioning. Use the cutting instructions above to identify which fabric pieces correspond to each template number.

3. Each block quadrant is made up of one pieced template A unit and one pieced template B unit. Lay out each quadrant as shown in **fig. 1** and sew together the two units. Press.

4. Sew together the four quadrants to complete the block (**fig. 2**). Press.

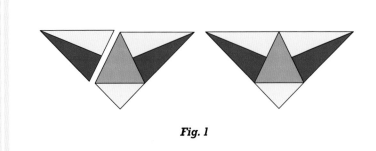

Fig. 1

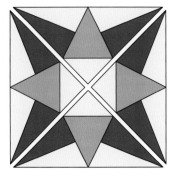

Fig. 2

MAKE THE STAR
BRIGHT QUILT

Materials

All fabric amounts are for 45" (114.5 cm) wide fabric.

- 2 yd (1.8 m) white fabric
- 1²/₃ yd (1.5 m) *total* of cool-color print fabrics (green, blue, and purple)
- 1¹/₂ yd (137 cm) *total* of warm-color print fabrics (red, orange, and yellow)
- 1²/₃ yd (1.5 m) light putty fabric
- 1¹/₈ yd (103 cm) dark putty fabric
- 4 yd (3.7 m) backing fabric
- 68" × 80" (152.5 × 203.2 cm) low-loft cotton batting
- ⅝ yd (57 cm) binding fabric

Tools

- Exploding Star Templates A and B*
- Foundation-piecing paper

* You will need to print fifty-two copies of each Exploding Star Template at 100 percent.

Cutting

FROM WHITE FABRIC, CUT:

❒ 26 squares 5" × 5" (12.5 × 12.5 cm); cut in half diagonally to make 52 half-square triangles (template piece A4).

❒ 78 rectangles 3¹/₂" × 7" (9 × 18 cm) (template pieces A2 and B2).

FROM COOL-COLOR FABRICS, CUT:

❒ 56 rectangles 3¹/₂" × 7" (9 × 18 cm) (template pieces A1 and B1).

❒ 28 rectangles 5" × 6" (12.5 × 15 cm) (template piece A3).

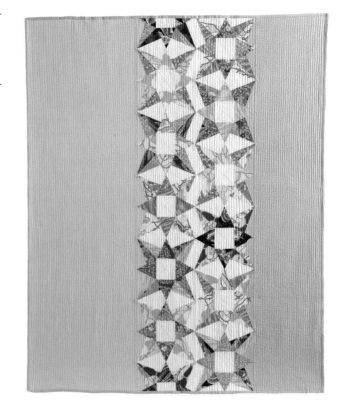

FROM WARM-COLOR FABRICS, CUT:

❒ 48 rectangles 3¹/₂" × 7" (9 × 18 cm) (template pieces A1 and B1).

❒ 24 rectangles 5" × 6" (12.5 × 15 cm) (template piece A3).

FROM LIGHT PUTTY FABRIC, CUT:

❒ 2 rectangles 22¹/₂" (57 cm) × width of fabric.

❒ 14 rectangles 3¹/₂" × 7" (9 × 18 cm) (template pieces A2 and B2).

FROM DARK PUTTY FABRIC, CUT:

❒ 2 rectangles 14¹/₂" (37 cm) × width of fabric.

❒ 12 rectangles 3¹/₂" × 7" (9 × 18 cm) (template pieces A2 and B2).

FROM BINDING FABRIC, CUT:

❒ 7 strips 2¹/₂" (6.5 cm) × width of fabric.

Exploding Star Blocks

UNFINISHED BLOCK:
12½" × 12½" (31.5 × 31.5 cm)

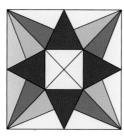

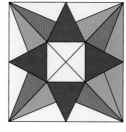

Follow the Classic Exploding Star block instructions to make thirteen blocks. Piece four cool-color and three warm-color stars using a light putty background along one block side (template pieces A2 and B2). Piece three cool-color and three warm-color stars using a dark putty background along one block side (template pieces A2 and B2). Use the cutting instructions to identify which fabric pieces correspond to each template number and note color value placement within the blocks.

Quilt Top

1 Lay out the blocks in two staggered columns as shown (*fig. 3*). Column 1 contains seven blocks, and column 2 contains six blocks. Alternate warm and cool colors and note the position of background colors.

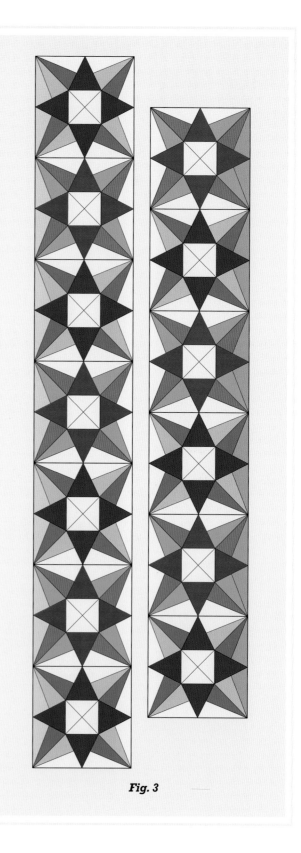

Fig. 3

2 Trim the top and bottom stars from the left column to 6½" × 12½" (16.5 × 31.5 cm) *(fig. 4)*. This will allow for the extra seam allowance needed due to the staggering of the blocks. Discard the smaller portions.

3 Sew together the stars into columns. Press. Sew the columns together, aligning the star points at the corners. Press seams open to reduce bulk.

4 Sew together the short ends of the two light putty rectangles 22½" (57 cm) × width of fabric. Trim to 22½" × 72½" (57 × 184.2 cm).

5 Sew the light putty rectangle 22½" × 72½" (57 × 184.2 cm) to the left of the star columns as shown in the Star Bright Construction Diagram.

6 Sew together the short ends of the two dark putty rectangles 14½" (37 cm) × width of fabric. Trim to 14 ½" × 72 ½" (37 × 184.2 cm).

7 Sew the dark putty rectangle 14½" × 72½" (37 × 184.2 cm) to the right of the star column. Press the seams open to reduce bulk.

8 Make a quilt sandwich with the backing, batting, and quilt top. Baste the layers and quilt as desired. I quilted a simple design of parallel lines that looks very modern. Trim the batting and backing to match the quilt top.

9 Join the binding strips to make a continuous length. Bind the raw edges to finish the quilt.

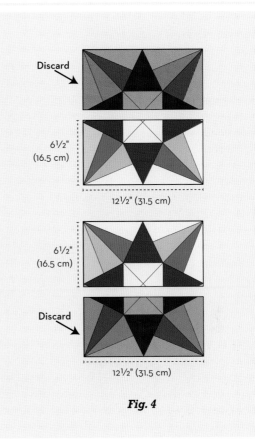

Fig. 4

MINI HISTORY LESSON:
Foundation Piecing

Foundation piecing, or paper piecing as it is also called, was historically used as a way of stabilizing fabric pieced together. Rather than using paper as the foundation, other scrap fabric was used. Foundation piecing may date back prior to the nineteenth century, but it has gained momentum and popularity in modern times. The ability to piece complicated quilt blocks easily and with perfect precision has excited many quilters. As modern technology has advanced, exact patterns can be printed or copied at home rather than hand drawn or stamped repeatedly, putting the ability to access these designs instantly at quilters' fingertips.

Star Bright Construction Diagram

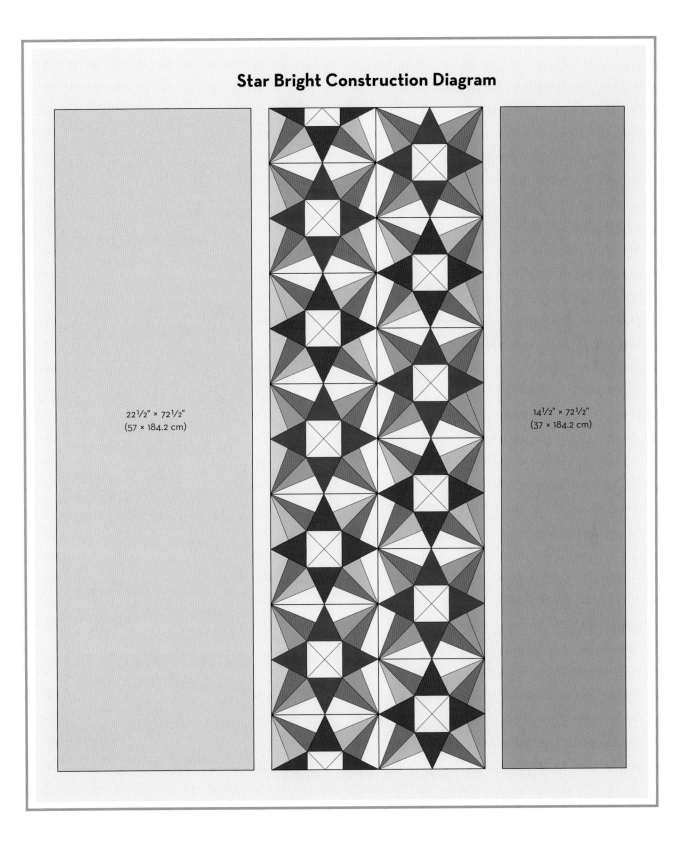

22½" × 72½"
(57 × 184.2 cm)

14½" × 72½"
(37 × 184.2 cm)

Geometric Star

Cut Glass Baby Quilt

*Designed and made by **Katie Clark Blakesley***

FINISHED SIZE:	TECHNIQUE USED:	SKILL LEVEL:
36" × 36" (91.5 × 91.5 cm)	Foundation piecing	Advanced

DESIGN NOTE:	*Sewing with Solid Fabrics*

In the early 2000s, solid fabrics exploded onto the quilting scene. Consequently, quilters can choose from a dizzying array of solid and semi-solid fabrics, each with different sheens, hands, weaves, and their own distinct "look." Semi-solid prints, such as cross-weaves, yarn-dyed linen/cotton blends, shot cottons, and voiles further round out the solids market. Manufacturers offer "color cards," similar to paint chips, which can help ensure that you purchase just the right solid for your project.

Solid fabrics are a staple for many quilters, and in a complicated design like this one, with twenty-eight pieces in each block, solids shine. Add something unexpected to an all-solids quilt. Here, a solitary orange print is used as a "pop" of color, and a darker fabric, used sparingly, adds depth. Creative shading with color in some of the blocks imparts a stunning secondary design that makes a great wall hanging or baby quilt.

Katie Clark Blakesley

CLASSIC GEOMETRIC STAR BLOCK

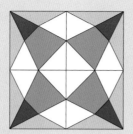

UNFINISHED BLOCK:
12½" × 12½" (31.5 × 31.5 cm)

Choose scraps from your stash to make this classic version for a block swap or bee. If you want to make it for a sampler quilt, see pages 146–157. To make the Cut Glass Baby Quilt version, see opposite page. Geometric Star Templates A, B, and C are on the CD included with this book.

Cutting

FROM TURQUOISE FABRIC, CUT:

- ❏ 4 rectangles 4" × 5" (10 × 12.5 cm) (template piece A1).

FROM WHITE FABRIC, CUT:

- ❏ 2 squares 5" × 5" (12.5 × 12.5 cm) cut in half diagonally to make 4 half-square triangles (template piece A3).

- ❏ 8 rectangles 4" × 4" (10 × 10 cm) (template pieces B2 and C2).

FROM CORAL FABRIC, CUT:

- ❏ 4 rectangles 3½" × 4½" (9 × 11.5 cm) (template piece A2).

FROM GRAY FABRIC, CUT:

- ❏ 8 strips 3" × 8" (7.5 × 20.5 cm) (template pieces C1 and B1).

Assembling the Block

1. Print and cut out four copies of *each* Geometric Star Template at 100 percent.

2. Using the technique described in Guide to Foundation Piecing (page 13), piece twelve templates. Use the cutting instructions above to identify which fabric pieces correspond to each template number.

3. Lay out each set of pieced A, B, and C templates as shown in *fig. 1*. Sew together each set for a total of four units. Press.

4. Sew together the top two units and the bottom two units. Press. Sew together the top and bottom halves *(fig. 2)*. Press.

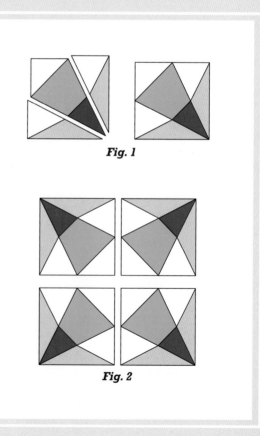

Fig. 1

Fig. 2

MAKE THE CUT GLASS BABY QUILT

Materials

All fabric amounts are for 45" (114.5 cm) wide fabric.

- 1¼ yd (114.5 cm) white fabric
- 1⅜ yd (125.5 cm) gray solid fabric
- ½ yd (45.5 cm) coral solid fabric
- 1 fat quarter (18" × 22") (45.5 × 56 cm) or scraps of orange print fabric
- ⅝ yd (57 cm) turquoise solid fabric
- ⅜ yd (34.5 cm) dark turquoise solid fabric
- 1¼ yd (114.5 cm) backing fabric
- 40" × 40" (101.5 × 101.5 cm) low-loft cotton batting
- ½ yd (45.5 cm) binding fabric

Tools

- Geometric Star Templates A, B, and C*
- Foundation-piecing paper

* You will need to cut out thirty-six copies of each Geometric Star Template at 100 percent.

Cutting

FROM WHITE FABRIC, CUT:

❐ 18 pieces 5" × 5" (12.5 × 12.5 cm) cut in half diagonally to make 36 half-square triangles (template piece A3).

❐ 56 rectangles 4" × 4" (10 × 10 cm) (template pieces B2 and C2).

FROM GRAY FABRIC, CUT:

❐ 72 strips 2½" × 8" (6.5 × 20.5 cm) (template pieces B1 and C1).

FROM CORAL FABRIC, CUT:

❐ 32 rectangles 3½" × 4½" (9 × 11.5 cm) (template piece A2).

FROM ORANGE PRINT FABRIC, CUT:

❐ 4 rectangles 3½" × 4½" (9 × 11.5 cm) (template piece A2).

FROM TURQUOISE FABRIC, CUT:

❐ 36 rectangles 4" × 5" (10 × 12.5 cm) (template piece A1).

FROM DARK TURQUOISE FABRIC, CUT:

❐ 16 rectangles 4" × 5" (10 × 12.5 cm) (template piece B2 and C2).

FROM BINDING FABRIC, CUT:

❐ 4 strips 2½" (6.5 cm) × width of fabric.

Geometric Star Blocks

UNFINISHED BLOCK: 12 1/2" × 12 1/2"
(31.5 × 31.5 cm)

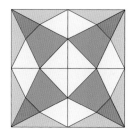

Make nine blocks.

In this quilt, five blocks are identical, and the other four (in the bottom right quadrant of the quilt) are shaded with darker turquoise pieces and an orange corner accent.

1 Follow the Classic Geometric Star block instructions to make five identical blocks using turquoise, coral, gray, and white fabrics. Use the cutting instructions to identify which fabric pieces correspond to each template number.

2 Follow the same instructions to make the remaining four blocks, but make them with some dark turquoise and orange pieces, as shown in **fig. 3**.

> ### Tip
> *If you have removed the paper at this stage, reduce your stitch length slightly to ensure that edge seams don't come apart.*

Quilt Top

1 Refer to the Cut Glass Construction Diagram to lay out the blocks in three rows of three blocks each. Sew together the blocks in rows, aligning seams. Press. Sew together the rows. Press.

2 Make a quilt sandwich with the backing, batting, and quilt top. Baste the layers and quilt as desired. I used a combination of outline and filler quilting. Trim the batting and backing to match the quilt top.

3 Join the binding strips to make a continuous length. Bind the raw edges to finish the quilt.

4 If you want to hang it on the wall, use your favorite method to add a hanging sleeve on the back.

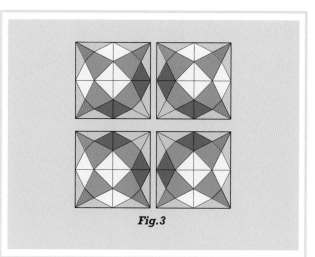

Fig. 3

MINI HISTORY LESSON:
Ladies Art Company

The Geometric Star block is found in *The Romance of the Patchwork Quilt in America*, written by Carrie A. Hall and Rose G. Kretsinger, and it was published in Caldwell, Idaho, in 1935. The Ladies Art Company, popularly acknowledged as the first mail-order pattern business, published a simpler version of the block before 1895: Pattern 199 "The Priscilla." The LAC, as it was known, was located in St. Louis, Missouri. It was the first to publish a quilt pattern catalog; in 1897 the catalog listed more than four hundred quilt patterns. The patterns, printed on tissue paper, at one time cost 10 cents each, three for 25 cents, or seven for 50 cents. In the 1930s, at the height of popularity for mail-order patterns, the Ladies Art Company employed more than fifty people.

Cut Glass Construction Diagram

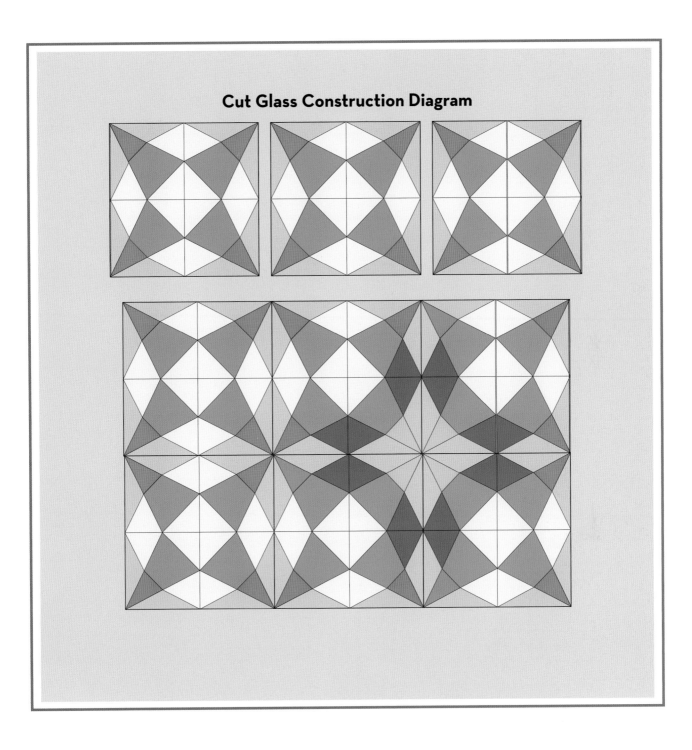

BLOCK:
Double Windmill

PROJECT:
Double Dutch Table Runner

*Designed and made by **Katie Clark Blakesley***

FINISHED SIZE:	TECHNIQUES USED:	SKILL LEVEL:
12" × 48" (31.5 × 123 cm)	Foundation piecing, partial seams	Intermediate

DESIGN NOTE:	*Highlighting One Block*

The Double Windmill pattern works very well with a variety of prints—it's the perfect stash or scrap project, since the amount of fabric needed is minimal. Combining solids and prints in a fresh color palette alters the look of this very traditional design. Changing the fabric choices in a single block adds something unexpected.

The quilting helps to add interest to this project. Quilting is a necessary part of pieced projects and can be used to create movement and interest in an otherwise predictable piece. Simply changing one or more variables—thread color and weight, hand or machine quilting, using straight lines or free-motion quilting, random or planned designs—can greatly enhance your project. In this case, radiating lines highlight the double windmill, while simpler quilting unifies the background areas. Some areas are left entirely unquilted, allowing them to "pop."

Katie Clark Blakesley

CLASSIC DOUBLE WINDMILL BLOCK

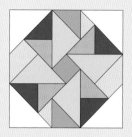

UNFINISHED BLOCK:
12½" × 12½" (31.5 × 31.5 cm)

Choose scraps from your stash to make this classic version for a block swap or bee. If you want to make it for a sampler quilt, see pages 146–157. To make the Double Dutch Table Runner version, see page 122. Double Windmill templates A and B are on the CD included with this book.

Cutting

FROM ORANGE FABRIC, CUT:

❒ 2 squares 5" × 5" (12.5 × 12.5 cm); cut in half diagonally to make 4 half-square triangles (template pieces A1 and B1).

FROM RED FABRIC, CUT:

❒ 2 squares 5" × 5" (12.5 × 12.5 cm); cut in half diagonally to make 4 half-square triangles (template pieces A2 and B2).

FROM YELLOW FABRIC, CUT:

❒ 2 squares 6" × 6" (15 × 15 cm); cut in half diagonally to make 4 half-square triangles (template pieces A3 and B3).

FROM CREAM FABRIC, CUT:

❒ 1 square 5" × 5" (12.5 × 12.5 cm); cut in half diagonally to make 2 half-square triangles (template pieces A5).

❒ 2 rectangles 2½" × 4" (5.5 × 10 cm) (template B4).

FROM GREEN FABRIC, CUT:

❒ 1 square 3½" × 3½" (9 × 9 cm); cut in half diagonally to make 2 half-square triangles (template piece A4).

FROM AQUA FABRIC, CUT:

❒ 1 square 2⅝" × 2⅝" (6.75 × 6.75 cm).

FROM WHITE FABRIC, CUT:

❒ 2 squares 5½" × 5½" (14 × 14 cm); cut in half diagonally to make 4 half-square triangles.

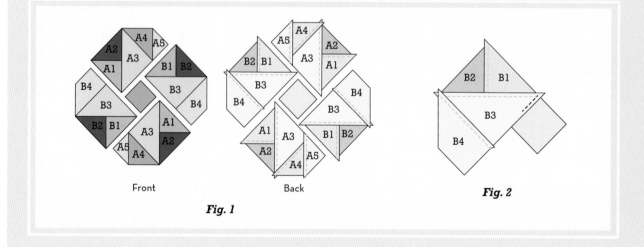

Front   Back   *Fig. 2*

Fig. 1

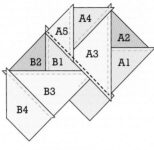

Fig. 3

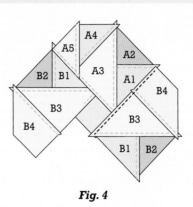

Fig. 4

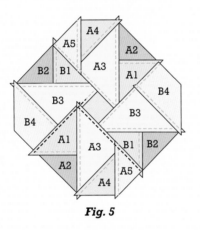

Fig. 5

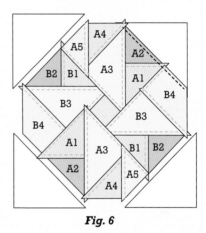

Fig. 6

Assembling the Block

1. Print and cut out two copies of *each* Double Windmill Template at 100 percent.

2. Using the technique described in Guide to Foundation Piecing (page 13), piece four templates. Use the cutting instructions to identify which fabric pieces correspond to each template number.

3. Lay out the four pieced units as shown in *fig. 1*, with the aqua square in the center.

4. Use the technique described in Guide to Partial Seams (page 14) to sew the pieced units to the center square. Remember that the illustrations show the back side of the fabric.

5. Sew the right unit to the center square using a partial seam *(fig. 2)*. Sew on the top unit using a regular seam *(fig. 3)* and do the same with the left unit *(fig. 4)*. Use a regular seam on the first side and then a partial seam to sew on the final unit *(fig. 5)*.

6. Sew on the white corner triangles *(fig. 6)*. Press and trim to 12½" × 12½" (31.5 × 31.5 cm), if necessary.

MAKE THE DOUBLE DUTCH TABLE RUNNER

Materials

All fabric amounts are for 45" (114.5 cm) wide fabric.

Note: *For a scrappy look, use scraps in a variety of prints of each color instead of a fat quarter (18" × 22") (45.5 × 56 cm) of one print.*

- 1 fat quarter of citron print fabric
- 1 fat quarter of dark gray print fabric
- 1 fat quarter of light gray print fabric
- 1 fat quarter of dark gray solid fabric
- 1 fat quarter of coral print fabric
- 1 square 2⅝" × 2⅝" (6.75 × 6.75 cm) of white solid fabric
- ½ yd (45.5 cm) light gray solid fabric
- 1 yd (91.5 cm) 40.5 × 132 cm) backing fabric
- 16" × 52" (40.5 × 132 cm) low-loft cotton batting
- ⅓ yd (30.5 cm) binding fabric

Tools

- Double Windmill templates A and B*
- Foundation-piecing paper

* *You will need to print eight copies of each Double Windmill Template at 100 percent.*

Cutting

FROM CITRON PRINT FABRIC, CUT:

- ❐ 6 squares 5" × 5" (12.5 × 12.5 cm); cut in half diagonally to make 12 half-square triangles (template pieces A1 and B1).

FROM DARK GRAY PRINT FABRIC, CUT:

- ❐ 8 squares 5" × 5" (12.5 × 12.5 cm); cut in half diagonally to make 16 half-square triangles (template pieces A2 and B2).

FROM LIGHT GRAY PRINT FABRIC, CUT:

- ❐ 6 squares 6" × 6" (15 × 15 cm); cut in half diagonally to make 12 half-square triangles (template pieces A3 and B3).

- ❐ 2 squares 5" × 5" (12.5 × 12.5 cm); cut in half diagonally to make 4 half-square triangles (template pieces A1 and B1).

FROM DARK GRAY SOLID FABRIC, CUT:

- ❐ 4 squares 5" × 5" (12.5 × 12.5 cm); cut in half diagonally to make 8 half-square triangles (template pieces A4).

- ❐ 4 squares 3½" × 3½" (9 × 9 cm); cut in half diagonally to make 8 half-square triangles (template piece A5).

- ❐ 8 rectangles 2½" × 4" (6.5 × 10 cm) (template piece B4).

FROM CORAL FABRIC, CUT:

- ❐ 3 squares 2⅝" × 2⅝" (6.75 × 6.75 cm).

- ❐ 2 squares 6" × 6" (15 × 15 cm); cut in half diagonally to make 4 half-square triangles (template pieces A3 and B3).

FROM WHITE SOLID FABRIC, CUT:

- ❐ 1 square 2⅝" × 2⅝" (6.75 × 6.75 cm).

FROM LIGHT GRAY SOLID FABRIC, CUT:

- ❐ 8 squares 5½" × 5½" (14 × 14 cm); cut in half diagonally to make 16 half-square triangles (corner squares).

FROM BINDING FABRIC, CUT:

- ❐ 4 strips 2½" (6.5 cm) × width of fabric.

Double Windmill Blocks

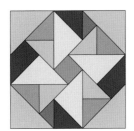

UNFINISHED BLOCK:
12½" × 12½" (31.5 × 31.5 cm)

Make three blocks the same and one accent block.

Follow the Classic Double Windmill block instructions to make three blocks using the citron fabric for pieces A1 and B1 and coral for the center. Make a fourth block using the light gray print fabric for A1 and B1, white for the center, and coral for A3 and B3.

Table Runner

1 Refer to the Table Runner Construction Diagram to lay out the four blocks. Sew the blocks together.

2 Make a quilt sandwich with the backing, batting, and runner top. Baste the layers and quilt as desired. I quilted some areas of the runner and left others unquilted, to make them "pop." Trim the batting and backing to match the runner top.

3 Join the binding strips to make a continuous length. Bind the raw edges to finish the runner.

MINI HISTORY LESSON:
Documenting Our Craft

Keeping a record of details about quilts you make is important. Because not every quilter labels her or his quilts or leaves behind detailed information about the fabric, pattern, and techniques used to create the quilts, the provenance of many quilts—both historic and contemporary—has been lost. Several organizations work to preserve quilts and the stories behind them. As a quiltmaker, consider participating in The Quilt Alliance's oral history project, Quilter's S.O.S. (Save our Stories), at www.allianceforamericanquilts.org. Fortunately, there are now many cultural resources for quilting, from local historical societies and museums to quilt festivals and shows around the world to temporary exhibitions in large venues. (For example, 2011 was the Year of the Quilt at the American Folk Art Museum in New York City.) To get an introduction to the world of quilt education and research, browse the Quilt Index (www.quiltindex.org) and the International Quilt Study Center's online offerings (www.quiltstudy.org).

Table Runner Construction Diagram

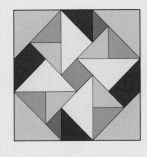  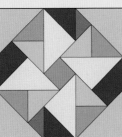 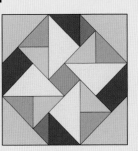

RE-IMAGINED BLOCKS

While updated colors and settings are wonderful ways to modernize a traditional block, consider taking it even further by changing the very design of the block itself. Whether it's making small modifications to simplify the piecing; attempting an improvised, "wonky" version of a traditional design; or an even more substantial update, traditional blocks can serve as a great jumping-off point for a design that may eventually become your own original creation.

BLOCK:

Dove at the Window

PROJECT:

Twinkle Mini Quilt

Designed and made by **Lee Heinrich**

FINISHED SIZE:	TECHNIQUE USED:	SKILL LEVEL:
22" × 22" (56 × 56 cm)	Improvisational piecing	Beginner

DESIGN NOTE:	*Going Wonky*

A fun and easy way to modernize a traditional block is to make it improvisational and "wonky." Instead of the precise piecing usually found in traditional blocks, with this technique the block is intentionally pieced at odd angles and with inexact points, giving it a more freeform look. A star block such as Dove at the Window is perfect for this technique—wonkiness often seems to give stars extra twinkle.

Some people find it easier than others to create wonkiness. If you are one of the many who find it difficult to purposely piece things "wrong," it may help for you to think that there is no "wrong" in this type of piecing. Personally, I tend to be too timid with my wonkiness, and, if anything, I often wish I had made the angles more dramatic. So don't be afraid to go for broke—really wonk up that block! You'll be glad you did.

CLASSIC DOVE AT THE WINDOW BLOCK

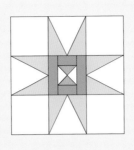

UNFINISHED BLOCK:
12½" × 12½" (31.5 × 31.5 cm)

Choose scraps from your stash to make this classic version for a block swap or bee. If you want to make it for a sampler quilt, see pages 146–157. To make the Twinkle Mini Quilt version, see page 130.

Cutting

FROM WHITE FABRIC, CUT:

❑ 4 squares 5" × 5" (12.5 × 12.5 cm).

❑ 4 squares 4½" × 4½" (11.5 × 11.5 cm).

❑ 1 square 3½" × 3½" (9 × 9 cm).

FROM YELLOW FABRIC, CUT:

❑ 8 rectangles 3" × 6" (7.5 × 15 cm).

FROM AQUA FABRIC, CUT:

❑ 2 rectangles 1½" × 2½" (3.8 × 3.8 cm).

❑ 2 strips 1½" × 4½" (3.8 × 11.5 cm).

FROM ORANGE FABRIC, CUT:

❑ 1 square 3½" × 3½" (9 × 9 cm).

Assembling the Block

1. To make star-point units, fold the four white squares 5" × 5" (12.5 × 12.5 cm) in half and press.

2. With the pieces still folded, cut each piece in half diagonally, from corner to corner, to make four triangles *(fig. 1)*. (The folded portions are the triangles you will use in the block.) Discard the scraps.

3. Unfold and sew a yellow rectangle 3" × 6" (7.5 × 15 cm) to each long edge of the triangle *(fig. 2)*.

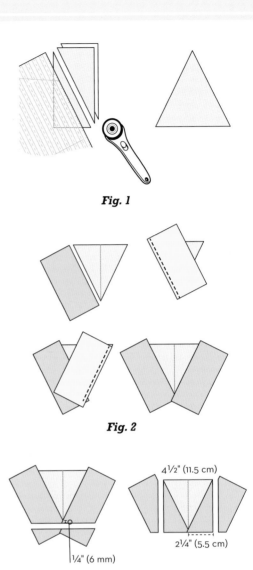

Fig. 1

Fig. 2

Fig. 3

4. Trim the unit to 4½" × 4½" (11.5 × 11.5 cm). Trim the bottom edge ¼" (6 mm) from the point of the triangle and trim each side 2¼" (5.5 cm) from the center crease. Then trim the top edge to square up to 4½" × 4½" (11.5 × 11.5 cm). Repeat with the other folded pieces to make four star-point units *(fig. 3)*.

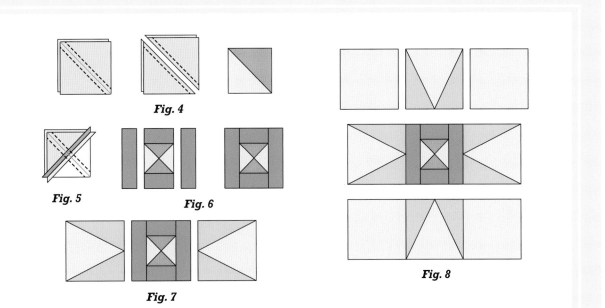

Fig. 4

Fig. 5

Fig. 6

Fig. 7

Fig. 8

Tip

Your star-point seams should not be a full ¼" (6 mm) from the top corners of the unit when trimmed to 4 ½" × 4 ½" (11.5 × 11.5 cm). This may look wrong at first glance, but it is correct!

5. To make the center unit, use a water-soluble pen or fabric marker to draw a line diagonally from corner to corner on the back of the orange square and pair it up with the white square, right sides together. Sew ¼" (6 mm) from the marked line on each side *(fig. 4)* to make half-square-triangle units. Cut along the marked diagonal line and press open. Align a 45-degree ruler marking with the center angled seam and trim the units to 3" × 3" (7.5 × 7.5 cm).

6. On one of the half-square-triangle units, draw a line diagonally from corner to corner on the back as shown *(fig. 5)*. With right sides together, pair up the half-square-triangle units, alternating colors. Sew ¼" (6 mm) from the marked line on each side.

7. Cut along the marked diagonal line and press open. Trim one of the resulting quarter-square-triangle units to 2½" × 2½" (6.5 × 6.5 cm). Discard the other quarter-square-triangle unit.

8. Sew the 1½" × 2½" (3.8 × 6.5 cm) aqua strips to the top and bottom of the trimmed quarter-square-triangle unit. Sew the 1½" × 4½" (3.8 × 11.5 cm) aqua strips to each side of the trimmed quarter-square-triangle unit to complete the block center *(fig. 6)*.

9. Sew a star-point unit onto each side of the center unit as shown *(fig. 7)* to make the middle block row. Press seams toward the center unit.

10. Sew a white square 4½" × 4½" (11.5 × 11.5 cm) to each side of the two remaining star-point units to make the block top and bottom rows. Press seams toward the outer corners. Sew together the three rows to complete the block *(fig. 8)*.

MAKE THE TWINKLE MINI QUILT

Materials

All fabric amounts are for 45" (114.5 cm) wide fabric.

- ¼ yd (23 cm) *each of two light yellow print fabrics*
- ¼ yd (23 cm) *each of two turquoise print fabrics*
- Scrap of turquoise print fabric, at least 3" × 6" (7.5 × 15 cm)
- ¼ yd (23 cm) *each of four red print fabrics*
- Scrap of gold print fabric, at least 3" × 6" (7.5 × 15 cm)
- ½ yd (45.5 cm) green print fabric
- ¾ yd (68.5 cm) backing fabric
- 26" × 26" (66 × 66 cm) low-loft cotton batting
- ¼ yd (23 cm) binding fabric

Cutting

FROM LIGHT YELLOW PRINT FABRICS, CUT:

❏ 8 squares 3¾" × 3¾" (9.5 × 9.5 cm).

❏ 8 squares 3½" × 3½" (9 × 9 cm).

FROM TURQUOISE PRINT FABRICS, CUT:

❏ 8 squares 3¾" × 3¾" (9.5 × 9.5 cm).

❏ 8 squares 3½" × 3½" (9 × 9 cm).

FROM TURQUOISE PRINT SCRAP, CUT:

❏ 2 squares 3" × 3" (7.5 × 7.5 cm).

FROM RED PRINT FABRICS, CUT:

❏ 32 rectangles 3" × 5½" (7.5 × 12.5 cm).

FROM GOLD PRINT FABRIC, CUT:

❏ 2 squares 3" × 3" (7.5 × 7.5 cm).

FROM GREEN PRINT FABRIC, CUT:

❏ 8 rectangles 1¼" × 2" (3.2 × 5 cm).

❏ 8 strips 2" × 4½" (5 × 11.5 cm).

❏ 2 strips 2½" × 18½" (6.5 × 47 cm).

❏ 2 strips 2½" × 22½" (6.5 × 57 cm).

FROM BINDING FABRIC, CUT:

❏ 3 strips 2½" (6.5 cm) × width of fabric.

Wonky Dove at the Window Block

UNFINISHED BLOCK:
9½" × 9½" (24 × 24 cm)

This block is made in the same way as the classic Dove at the Window Block, but the cuts are wonky instead of straight. Follow those instructions to make four blocks.

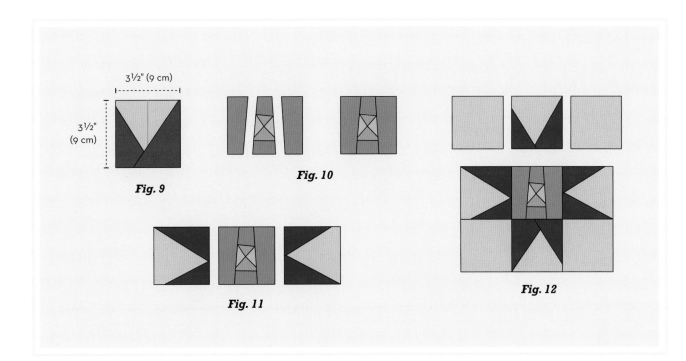

Fig. 9

Fig. 10

Fig. 11

Fig. 12

1 Using the same technique shown in the Classic Block instructions on page 128, fold in half, press, and cut the 3³⁄₄" × 3³⁄₄" (9.5 × 9.5 cm) light yellow and turquoise squares into four triangles, but make your cut wonky instead of straight. Unfold and sew a red rectangle to each long triangle edge.

2 Trim the unit to 3¹⁄₂" × 3¹⁄₂" (9 × 9 cm) square *(fig. 9)*. (Seam allowances for the star points do not have to be exact in your trimmed square.) Repeat with the other folded pieces, so that you have sixteen star-point units (eight with light yellow backgrounds and eight with turquoise backgrounds).

3 Draw an uneven diagonal line at an odd angle across the back of the turquoise square 3" × 3" (7.5 × 7.5 cm). Pair it with the gold square, right sides facing. Sew ¹⁄₄" (6 mm) from the marked line on each side to make a wonky half-square-triangle unit. Your sewing can be a bit wonky here, too! Cut along the line and press open. Trim as desired to achieve a wonky look, but the resulting square should be about 2¹⁄₂" × 2¹⁄₂" (6.5 × 6.5 cm).

4 On one of the half-square-triangle units, draw an uneven or wonky line diagonally from corner to corner on the back. With right sides together, pair up that half-square-triangle unit with the other half-square-triangle unit, alternating colors. Sew ¹⁄₄" (6 mm) from the marked line on each side. Cut along the line and press open. Trim one of the resulting quarter-square-triangle units to about 2" × 2" (5 × 5 cm).

5 Sew the green rectangles 1¹⁄₄" × 2" (3.2 × 5 cm) to the top and bottom of the quarter-square-triangle unit. Press and trim the sides of the unit at slight angles to make it wonky *(fig. 10)*. Sew the green strips 2" × 4¹⁄₂" (5 × 11.5 cm) to each side of the unit to complete the block center. (These strips are purposely oversized to give you extra room to create the wonkiness). Trim the unit to 3¹⁄₂" × 3¹⁄₂" (9 × 9 cm) square. (Trim the unit to exactly 3¹⁄₂" × 3¹⁄₂" (9 × 9 cm) to ensure an accurate finished block.) Sew a star-point unit onto each side of the center unit to make the middle row *(fig. 11)*.

6 Sew 3¹⁄₂" × 3¹⁄₂" (9 × 9 cm) light yellow/red and turquoise/red squares to each side of the remaining star-point units to make the top and bottom rows *(fig. 12)*. Sew together the three rows to complete the block. Keep these seams straight to ensure the completed block measures 9¹⁄₂" × 9¹⁄₂" (24 × 24 cm) square.

Quilt Top

1 Sew each block with a turquoise background to a block with a light yellow background. Sew the paired blocks together to create a four-patch mini-quilt top.

2 Sew the green strips 2½" × 18½" (6.5 × 47 cm) to the top and bottom of the quilt top and trim the border strips so they are even with the blocks.

3 Sew the green border strips 2½" × 22½" (6.5 × 57 cm) to the sides of the quilt top and square up the border strips to complete the top.

4 Make a quilt sandwich with the backing, batting, and quilt top. Baste the layers and quilt as desired. I quilted concentric circles, which provide an interesting contrast to the squares. Trim the batting and backing to match the quilt top.

5 Join the binding strips to make a continuous length. Bind the raw edges to finish the quilt.

6 If you want to hang it on the wall, use your favorite method to add a hanging sleeve on the back.

MINI HISTORY LESSON:
The Quilts of Gee's Bend

There may be no historic quilt genre that has more influence on the modern quilting movement than the quilts of Gee's Bend—a unique, bold, and graphic style of quilting centered in Gee's Bend, Alabama. The quilting tradition in this rural, predominantly African American community of 750 people may go back to the early 1800s, when the area was a cotton plantation worked by slaves. As early as the 1930s and 1940s, women in the area were piecing together scraps of clothing and old bedding to create strikingly artistic quilts. These quilts typically feature wonky blocks and squares, Log Cabin blocks, solid colors, and minimalist designs with lots of negative space—all design characteristics both of the Gee's Bend quilts and some of today's modern quilt designs.

Most Gee's Bend quilts are now created by the Gee's Bend Collective, which is made up of more than fifty local quiltmakers. Quilts made by the collective have sold for as much as $20,000. The quilts have been exhibited at the Whitney Museum of American Art and art museums in Philadelphia, Indianapolis, Houston, and others. In "Jazzy Geometry, Cool Quilters," *New York Times*, November 29, 2002, art critic Michael Kimmelman wrote that the Gee's Bend quilts "turn out to be some of the most miraculous works of modern art America has produced."

BLOCK:
Art Square

PROJECT:
Times Square Quilt

Designed and made by **Katie Clark Blakesley**

FINISHED SIZE:	TECHNIQUE USED:	SKILL LEVEL:
60" × 72" (152.5 × 182.9 cm)	Simple piecing	Beginner

DESIGN NOTE:	*Expanding a Block*

The simple Art Square quilt block consists of a center square set on-point and surrounded by triangles. Traditionally, multiple blocks are set side by side, with or without sashing. But here, for a modern look, I made a single large block that is the focal point of the quilt and is surrounded by negative space. The block itself is expanded using a Pineapple-block setting.

Pineapple-block designs start in the center and then certain design elements are repeated over and over, radiating outward. They are part of the Log Cabin family of blocks. Pineapple blocks are unique because, according to the International Quilt Study Center and Museum's website, the block is both horizontally and vertically symmetrical, so it looks the same no matter how it is rotated. In this case, the block starts with a center Art Square block; the design elements are mimicked by Flying Geese units surrounding the original block. I added only two additional rows all around, to keep the design graphic and simple. But this type of block construction could be adapted to transform the look of a number of simple blocks, with as many "pineapple" layers as the maker wishes.

This quilt is very versatile. Simply changing the size of the surrounding white fabric, or negative space, will affect not only the size but also the look of the quilt.

Katie Clark Blakesley

CLASSIC ART SQUARE BLOCK

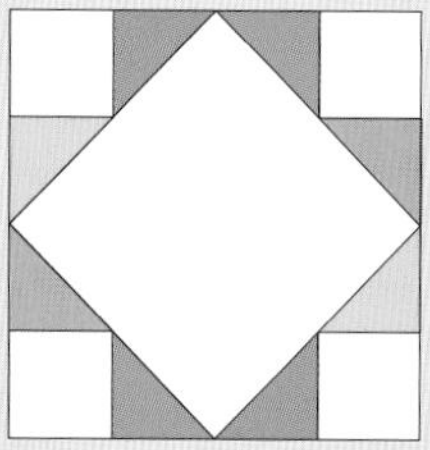

UNFINISHED BLOCK:
12½" × 12½" (31.5 × 31.5 cm)

Choose scraps from your stash to make this classic version for a block swap or bee. If you want to make it for a sampler quilt, see pages 146–157. To make the Times Square Quilt version, see opposite page.

Cutting

FROM YELLOW FABRIC, CUT:

❑ 1 square 3⅞" × 3⅞" (9.75 × 9.75 cm); cut in half diagonally to make 2 half-square triangles.

FROM ORANGE FABRIC, CUT:

❑ 1 square 3⅞" × 3⅞" (9.75 × 9.75 cm); cut in half diagonally to make 2 half-square triangles.

FROM AQUA FABRIC, CUT:

❑ 1 square 3⅞" × 3⅞" (9.75 × 9.75 cm); cut in half diagonally to make 2 half-square triangles.

FROM GREEN FABRIC, CUT:

❑ 1 square 3⅞" × 3⅞" (9.75 × 9.75 cm); cut in half diagonally to make 2 half-square triangles.

FROM WHITE FABRIC, CUT:

❑ 4 squares 3½" × 3½" (9 × 9 cm).

❑ 1 square 9" × 9" (23 × 23 cm).

Assembling the Block

1. Lay out the pieces as shown, arranging the colors as desired *(fig. 1)*.

2. To make the corners, place a colored half-square triangle and a white square 3½" × 3½" (9 × 9 cm) right sides together, lining up the upper right-hand corners as shown *(fig. 2)*, and sew them together along the right edge. Open and press seams toward

the darker triangle. Pair a second colored triangle with the square, lining up the left-hand corners as shown, and sew together at the lower edge. Open and press seams toward the darker triangle.

3. Repeat Steps 1 and 2 to make a total of four corner units, noting the triangle color placement.

4. Place the 9" × 9" (23 × 23 cm) white square on point and arrange the four corner units around it as desired. Sew one corner to one side of the square with the centers of the edges matching. The triangles will have about a ¼" (6 mm) of overhang on either side. Press. Repeat with the opposite corner and then the final two corners. Trim to square up the edges.

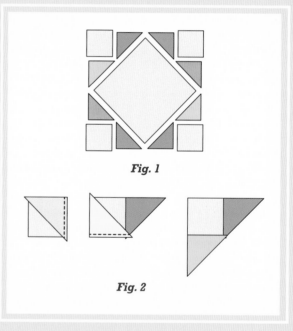

Fig. 1

Fig. 2

Tip

Bias edges stretch more than normal. Use spray starch or starch alternative to add some stability and pin carefully, taking care not to distort the edges.

MAKE THE TIMES SQUARE QUILT

Materials

All fabric amounts are for 45" (114.5 cm) wide fabric.

- 1 fat quarter (18" × 22") (45.5 × 56 cm) or equivalent scraps of various orange print fabrics
- 1 fat quarter (18" × 22") (45.5 × 56 cm) or equivalent scraps of various red print fabrics
- $\frac{1}{2}$ yd (45.5 cm) or equivalent scraps of various yellow print fabrics
- $3\frac{1}{2}$ yd (3.2 m) white solid fabric
- 4 yd (3.45 m) backing fabric
- 68" × 80" (172.7 × 203.2 cm) low-loft cotton batting
- $\frac{5}{8}$ yd (57 cm) binding fabric

Tools

- Water-soluble pen or other fabric marker

Cutting

FROM ORANGE PRINT FABRIC, CUT:

❒ 4 squares $3\frac{1}{4}$" × $3\frac{1}{4}$" (8.5 × 8.5 cm).

FROM RED PRINT FABRIC, CUT:

❒ 4 squares $5\frac{1}{4}$" × $5\frac{1}{4}$" (13.5 × 13.5 cm).

FROM YELLOW PRINT FABRIC, CUT:

❒ 4 squares $9\frac{1}{4}$" × $9\frac{1}{4}$" (23.5 × 23.5 cm).

FROM WHITE SOLID FABRIC, CUT:

Cut the following four pieces first on the lengthwise grain:

❒ 1 strip $8\frac{1}{4}$" × $32\frac{1}{2}$" (21 × 82.5 cm).

❒ 1 rectangle $20\frac{1}{4}$" × $32\frac{1}{2}$" (51.5 × 82.5 cm).

❒ 1 strip $6\frac{1}{4}$" × 60" (16 × 152.5 cm).

❒ 1 rectangle $34\frac{1}{4}$" × 60" (87 × 152.5 cm).

❒ 4 squares $9\frac{1}{4}$" × $9\frac{1}{4}$ " (23.5 × 23.5 cm).

❒ 4 squares $5\frac{1}{4}$" × $5\frac{1}{4}$" (13.5 × 13.5 cm).

❒ 4 squares $3\frac{1}{4}$" × $3\frac{1}{4}$" (8.5 × 8.5 cm).

❒ 4 squares $2\frac{1}{2}$" × $2\frac{1}{2}$" (6.5 × 6.5 cm).

❒ 5 squares $4\frac{1}{2}$" × $4\frac{1}{2}$" (11.5 × 11.5 cm).

❒ 4 squares $8\frac{1}{2}$" × $8\frac{1}{2}$" (21.5 × 21.5 cm).

FROM BINDING FABRIC, CUT:

❒ 7 strips $2\frac{1}{2}$" (6.5 cm) × width of fabric.

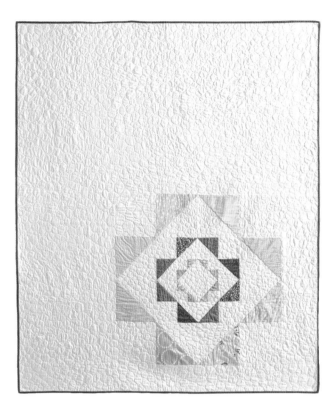

Art Square Block

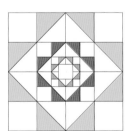

UNFINISHED BLOCK:
$32\frac{1}{2}$" × $32\frac{1}{2}$" (82.5 × 82.5 cm)

The single block for this quilt is made a little differently from the Classic Art Square block. Instead of cut half-square triangles, it's made with pieced half-square-triangle units, combined to make Flying Geese units. Start with the center orange-and-white block and build outward in "Pineapple block" fashion.

1 With a water-soluble pen or other fabric marker, draw a diagonal line on each of the white squares 9¼" × 9¼" (23.5 × 23.5 cm), 5¼" × 5¼" (13.5 × 13.5 cm), and 3¼" × 3¼" (8.5 × 8.5 cm).

2 To make the eight orange-and-white half-square-triangle units, place four white squares 3¼" × 3¼" (8.5 × 8.5 cm) right sides together with four orange squares 3¼" × 3¼" (8.5 × 8.5 cm). Sew ¼" (6 mm) on both sides of the marked line and cut on the drawn line *(fig. 3)*. Open and press the seams toward the darker fabric.

3 To square up the half-square-triangle units, line up the seam with the 45-degree ruler mark and trim to 2½" × 2½" (6.5 × 6.5 cm).

4 Repeat Steps 2 and 3 to make eight red-and-white half-square-triangle units using the four red and four white squares 5¼" × 5¼" (13.5 × 13.5 cm). Trim each to 4½" × 4½" (11.5 × 11.5 cm). Set aside.

5 Repeat Steps 2 and 3 to make eight yellow-and-white half-square-triangle units using the four yellow and four white squares 9¼" × 9¼" (23.5 × 23.5 cm). Trim each to 8½" × 8½" (21.5 × 21.5 cm). Set aside.

6 Lay out the center white square 4½" × 4½" (11.5 × 11.5 cm), the white squares 2½" × 2½" (6.5 × 6.5 cm), and the orange-and-white half-square-triangle units as shown in *fig. 4*.

7 Sew together the top row squares and half-square-triangle units. Press. Repeat with bottom row.

8 Sew the side half-square triangles together and sew them to the sides of the center square. Press.

9 Sew the three horizontal rows together. Press.

10 Repeat Steps 6 to 9 using the four white squares 4½" × 4½" (11.5 × 11.5 cm) and the eight red-and-white half-square-triangle units to add the next layer to the block.

11 Repeat Steps 6 to 9 using the four white squares and the eight yellow-and-white half-square-triangle units 8½" × 8½" (21.5 × 21.5 cm) and the white squares to add the outer layer to the block as shown in *fig. 5*.

Quilt Top

1 Lay out the four white "borders" as shown in the Times Square Construction Diagram. Sew the white rectangle 8¼" × 32½" (21 × 82.5 cm) to the right of the 32½" × 32½" (82.5 × 82.5 cm) Art Square block. Sew the white rectangle 20¼" × 32½" (51.5 × 82.5 cm) to the left of the block. Press.

2 Sew the white strip 6¼" × 60" (16 × 152.5 cm) to the bottom. Sew the white rectangle 34¼" × 60" to the top. Press and trim the quilt top if needed.

3 Make a quilt sandwich with the backing, batting, and quilt top. Baste the layers and quilt as desired. I used an allover bubble pattern. Trim the batting and backing to match the quilt top.

4 Join the binding strips to make a continuous length. Bind the raw edges to finish the quilt.

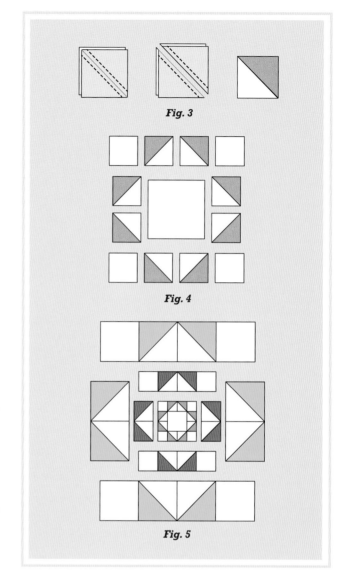

Fig. 3

Fig. 4

Fig. 5

Times Square Construction Diagram

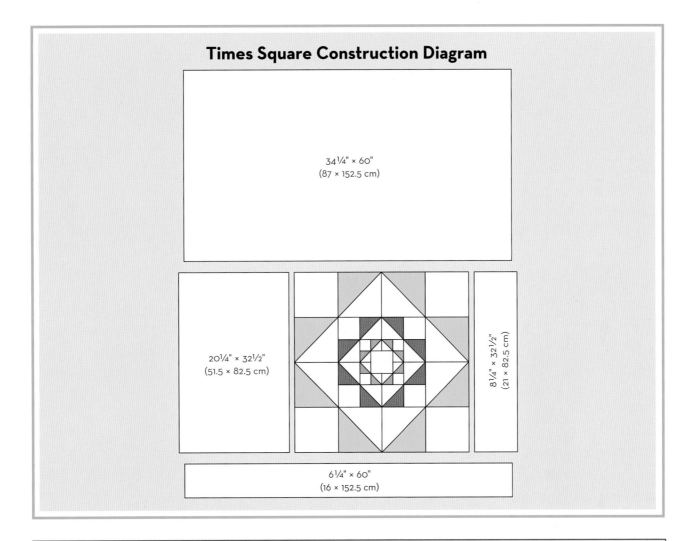

34¼" × 60"
(87 × 152.5 cm)

20¼" × 32½"
(51.5 × 82.5 cm)

8¼" × 32½"
(21 × 82.5 cm)

6¼" × 60"
(16 × 152.5 cm)

MINI HISTORY LESSON:
Community Quilts

Quilting bees, also known as "a quilting" began in the nineteenth century. A number of friends and/or neighbors gathered together and worked on blocks and quilt tops for each other. Most often, women sat together to handquilt a finished top that had been stretched over a sturdy homemade wood frame.

While making quilts is often a solitary undertaking, most quilters feel a need to connect with one another. In the past, contributing blocks to a wedding quilt or a quilting bee helped quilters learn from each other and enjoy one another's company.

Today, many quilters join quilting groups or more formal guilds for the same reasons: to find friendship, to learn from each other, to increase their skills, and to bring in speakers and put together quilt shows. Many quilters have found a similar community on the Internet, through blogs, photo-sharing websites, smart phone applications, and social media sites. They have participated in bees, shared their talents, and formed communities. And our guess is that quilting bees of the past were much like many guild meetings, retreats, and conferences of today in that socializing often takes precedent over sewing!

BLOCK:
Mosaic No. 8

PROJECT:
Rainbow Mosaic Pillow

*Designed and made by **Lee Heinrich***

FINISHED SIZE:	TECHNIQUE USED:	SKILL LEVEL:
18" × 18" (45.5 × 45.5 cm)	Foundation piecing	Intermediate

DESIGN NOTE:	*Using a Block's Grid to Develop a Design*

Need a starting point for design inspiration? Try using a block's grid to expand it outward from the center.

The Mosaic No. 8 Block uses a four-by-four piecing grid with a pinwheel at its center. For this pillow project, I added several more rows to the grid's outer ring and extended the lines of the block into these outer rows *(fig. 1)*. I then played with color placement and negative space until I had my Rainbow Mosaic design. In this case, a single block makes the pillow front.

This technique could be used with many other blocks as well. Drawing out blocks on graph paper can help you to see the block's grid and allow you to experiment with different ways of expanding the design outward.

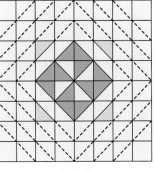

Fig. 1

CLASSIC MOSAIC NO. 8 BLOCK

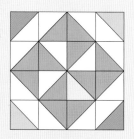

UNFINISHED BLOCK:
12½" × 12½" (31.5 × 31.5 cm)

Choose scraps from your stash to make this classic version for a block swap or bee. This block is traditionally made using half-square triangles. If you want to make it for a sampler quilt, see pages 146–157. To make the Rainbow Mosaic version, see opposite page.

Cutting

FROM WHITE FABRIC, CUT:

❑ 8 squares 4" × 4" (10 × 10 cm).

FROM AQUA FABRIC, CUT:

❑ 1 square 4" × 4" (10 × 10 cm).

FROM YELLOW FABRIC, CUT:

❑ 1 square 4" × 4" (10 × 10 cm).

FROM ORANGE FABRIC, CUT:

❑ 6 squares 4" × 4" (10 × 10 cm).

Assembling the Block

1. To make half-square-triangle units, use a water-soluble pen or fabric marker to mark each white square 4" × 4" (10 × 10 cm) with a diagonal line from corner to corner.

2. Pair each white square with an orange, aqua, or yellow square, right sides together.

3. Sew ¼" (6 mm) from the marked diagonal on both sides of the line *(fig. 2)*.

4. Cut each unit in half along the marked diagonal line. Press the half-square-triangle units open, pressing seam allowances open.

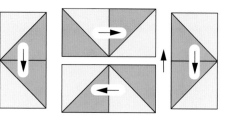

Fig. 2

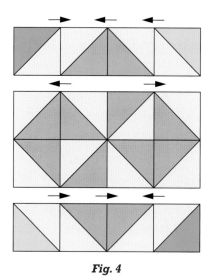

Fig. 3

Fig. 4

5. Align a 45-degree ruler line with the seam and trim the units to 3½" × 3½" (9 × 9 cm) square.

6. Piece the half-square-triangle units as shown, pressing seams in the direction of the arrows *(fig. 3 and fig. 4)*.

MAKE THE RAINBOW MOSAIC PILLOW

Materials

All fabric amounts are for 45" (114.5 cm) wide fabric.

- Brightly colored scraps, 2½" × 2½" to 6" × 6" (6.5 × 6.5 cm to 15 × 15 cm) for pillow top (I used eight different colors—blue, green, yellow-green, yellow, yellow-orange, orange, red-orange, and pink.)
- ½ yd (45.5 cm) white solid fabric
- ¼ yd (23 cm) gray print fabric for pillow binding
- ½ yd (45.5 cm) pillow back fabric
- 22" × 22" (56 × 56 cm) low-loft cotton batting
- 22" × 22" (56 × 56 cm) muslin
- 18" × 18" (45.5 × 45.5 cm) pillow form

Tools

- Rainbow Mosaic Pillow templates A, B, C, and D*
- Foundation-piecing paper
- Walking foot for sewing machine

** Print four copies of **each** Rainbow Mosaic Pillow Template at 100 percent.*

Cutting

FROM BLUE SCRAPS, CUT:

❒ 2 squares 3" × 3" (7.5 × 7.5 cm); cut in half diagonally to make 4 half-square triangles (template piece A1).

❒ 2 squares 2½" × 2½" (6.5 × 6.5 cm); cut in half diagonally to make 4 half-square triangles (template piece A3).

FROM GREEN SCRAPS, CUT:

❒ 4 squares 2½" × 2½" (6.5 × 6.5 cm); cut in half diagonally to make 8 half-square triangles (template pieces A5, A6).

FROM YELLOW-GREEN SCRAPS, CUT:

❒ 2 squares 2½" × 2½" (6.5 × 6.5 cm); cut in half diagonally to make 4 half-square triangles (template piece B1).

FROM YELLOW-ORANGE SCRAPS, CUT:

❒ 4 squares 2½" × 2½" (6.5 × 6.5 cm); cut in half diagonally to make 8 half-square triangles (template pieces B4, B5).

FROM YELLOW SCRAPS, CUT:

❒ 2 squares 3¾" × 3¾" (9.5 × 9.5 cm); cut in half diagonally to make 4 half-square triangles (template piece C1).

FROM ORANGE SCRAPS, CUT:

❒ 4 squares 4" × 4" (10 × 10 cm); cut in half diagonally to make 8 half-square triangles (template pieces C4, C5).

FROM RED-ORANGE SCRAPS, CUT:

❒ 2 squares 4" × 4" (10 × 10 cm); cut in half diagonally to make 4 half-square triangles (template piece D1).

FROM PINK SCRAPS, CUT:

❒ 2 squares 6" × 6" (15 × 15 cm); cut in half diagonally to make 4 half-square triangles (template piece D4).

FROM WHITE SOLID FABRIC, CUT:

❑ 2 squares 2½" × 2½" (6.5 × 6.5 cm); cut in half diagonally to make 4 half-square triangles (template piece A2).

❑ 4 strips 2" × 4½" (5 × 11.5 cm) (template piece A4).

❑ 8 squares 3¼" × 3¼" (8.5 × 8.5 cm) (template pieces B2, B3).

❑ 8 rectangles 2½" × 4½" (6.5 × 11.5 cm) (template pieces C2, C3).

❑ 8 rectangles 3½" × 6½" (9 × 16.5 cm) (template pieces D2, D3).

❑ 2 strips 2" × 15½" (5 × 39.5 cm).

❑ 2 strips 2" × 18½" (5 × 47 cm).

FROM PILLOW BACK FABRIC, CUT:

❑ 1 rectangle 14" × 18½" (35.5 × 47 cm).

❑ 1 strip 9" × 18½" (23 × 47 cm).

FROM BINDING FABRIC, CUT:

❑ 2 strips 2½" (6.5 cm) × width of fabric.

Mosaic No. 8 Pillow Top Block

Unlike the Classic Mosaic No. 8 block, this expanded version is made using foundation piecing. Make one block.

1 Using the technique described in Guide to Foundation Piecing (page 13), piece four of *each* template. Use the cutting instructions above to identify the fabric pieces that correspond to each template number.

2 Join one A, B, C, and D section to create a quarter-block *(fig. 5)*. Repeat with the other three sets. Press.

3 Join the quarter-blocks together *(fig. 6)* and press.

4 Sew one white strip 2" × 15½" (5 × 39.5 cm) to the top and bottom sides of pieced block.

5 Sew 1 white strip 2" × 18½" (5 × 47 cm) to each side to complete the top of the pillow. Press.

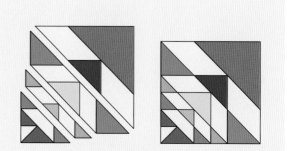

Fig. 5

Fig. 6

Tip

When sewing section D2 to D1 and section D3 to D1, align the long edge of the 3½" × 6½" (9 × 16.5 cm) D2/D3 white pieces with the edges of section D1. This may be counterintuitive, but it's necessary for piecing the block correctly.

Pillow Construction

1 Make a quilt sandwich with the muslin, batting, and pillow top. Baste the layers and quilt as desired. I chose to quilt straight lines that echo the pieced seaming.

2 On each of the two pillow back pieces, fold under one long edge 1/2" (1.3 cm) twice and press. Topstitch 1/4" (6 mm) from the folded edges to secure the hems.

3 Lay out the quilted pillow top, right side down. (This pillow cover is sewn wrong sides together—the binding added in Step 5 will hide the side seam allowances). Lay one of the pillow back pieces onto the pillow top, right side up and with bottom edges aligned. Lay the other pillow back piece on top of both, right side up with top edges aligned. The back pieces will overlap *(fig. 7)*. Pin all three layers.

4 Using a walking foot, sew around all sides 1/8" (3 mm) from the edge.

5 Join the binding strips to make a continuous length. Bind the raw edges as you would with a quilt to finish the pillow cover.

6 Insert the pillow form.

MINI HISTORY LESSON:
The Pinwheel Block

The pinwheel is one of the oldest pieced quilt blocks, dating back to the 1790s. Before that, most quilts were whole cloth or appliqué. The first pieced blocks (pinwheels among them) were generally used in borders surrounding a center medallion or as corner blocks. But it didn't take long for pieced blocks to become the primary focus of quilting designs, and the pinwheel has been a popular choice ever since.

It's no surprise: Pinwheels offer easy piecing, incredible versatility, and dynamic design. Endless variations on the basic pinwheel were in steady use by the mid-1800s. There were double pinwheels, multiple pinwheels arranged into patterns, pinwheels combined with patchwork, pinwheels within stars, and many more. It's not hard to see why quilters have returned to the pinwheel again and again over time.

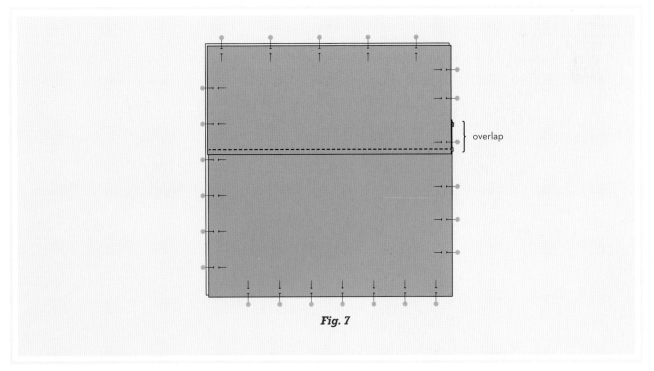

overlap

Fig. 7

SAMPLER QUILTS

Traditionally, a sampler quilt is made up of pieced or appliquéd blocks, no two of which have the same design. Although the individual blocks are all different, sometimes samplers are created around a theme of pattern or color. A sampler quilt might include different blocks all in the same genre, such as stars, paper-pieced blocks, or variations on a Nine Patch. Similarly, samplers can be organized around a specific fabric selection. For example, the fabrics may be all solids, all reproduction prints, or all from a single fabric designer or collection.

Sampler quilts started as a uniquely American quilt form. Before the 1830s and 1840s, most European and American quilts were in the medallion style, with a quilt pattern starting in the center and radiating outward. In the mid-nineteenth century, block-based quilts, oriented on a grid, became popular. They were appealing because the maker could work on one small block at a time. Quiltmakers could easily share quilt patterns (and blocks) with friends. Block-based quilts also made it easy for several quilters to contribute to a single quilt.

Traditionally, a sampler quilt is made up of pieced or appliquéd blocks, no two of which have the same design.

Sampler quilts were especially popular in Philadelphia, which is known for its pieced samplers, and in Baltimore, which is known for its intricate appliquéd Baltimore Album quilts (so-called because each participant signed her block, as was done in paper albums of an earlier era). One of the earliest existing sampler quilts (circa 1842–1843) was made by a Quaker woman from Philadelphia named Charlotte Gillingham. Her quilt measured 97" × 126" (246.4 × 320 cm) and included fifty-seven blocks, set on-point—a common Quaker quilt layout at the time.

Sampler quilts were made as wedding gifts, sold at fund-raisers, or given to important people in the community. Their popularity has waxed and waned over the past 170 years, with a recent rise in popularity.

This section of the book features three sampler quilts—one made by Lee, one by Katie, and one by Faith. All three quilts use the same classic blocks—the ones presented in the foregoing projects. But in each, small changes in color, setting, orientation, borders, and quilting result in three very different quilts.

SAMPLER QUILT IN A FABRIC COLLECTION

Designed and made by **Lee Heinrich**
Quilted by **Jenny Pedigo**

FINISHED SIZE: 59" × 75" (150 × 190.5 cm)

TECHNIQUES USED: Foundation piecing, partial seams

SKILL LEVEL: Intermediate

DESIGN NOTE: Borders and Binding

Borders and binding are an important way to set off sampler blocks, especially when sashing is not used, as is the case here. While I love the busy feel of the sampler blocks when put next to each other without sashing, I think it's important to give the eye somewhere to rest. The wide, solid white borders provide some much-needed negative space, and they have a calming effect that this design needs.

To finish it off, I knew I wanted to go back to bold and colorful, as a callback to the color chaos within the blocks. That's where the scrappy binding comes in. It's easy for binding to become an afterthought, since it's the last step in the long process of creating a quilt. But don't let fatigue cause you to ignore this important design element. Binding serves as the frame (or lack thereof) for your entire design. It may be narrow, but it can be the finishing touch that makes or breaks the entire quilt.

This sampler is made entirely from a single collection of fabric: Madrona Road, designed by Violet Craft for Michael Miller Fabrics. Sticking with just one line can help unify sampler blocks, since single lines have well-coordinated palettes and prints that play nicely together. But using only one line can also be challenging—some collections lend themselves to samplers better than others do. Look for lines with lots of small-scale prints, a strong palette, and not too much emphasis on multicolored prints (which can cause the design of a block to get a little lost).

Note: *Because manufacturers tend to offer any given fabric line for a relatively short time, the particular fabrics I used may no longer be available.*

Make the Sampler Quilt in a Single Fabric Collection

Fabric amounts and instructions for all twenty classic blocks can be found throughout this book. Refer to the visual block index on page 9 for specific page locations.

Materials

All fabric amounts are for 45" (114.5 cm) wide fabric.

- Fabric as needed for the selected twenty sampler blocks
- 1⅞ yd (1.7 m) white solid border fabric
- 3⅔ yd (3.36 m) backing fabric
- 66" × 82" (167.7 × 208.3 cm) low-loft cotton batting
- Scraps from piecing the sampler blocks for binding

Tools

- Template patterns for foundation-pieced blocks
- Foundation-piecing paper
- Hera marker or water-soluble pen

Cutting

From sampler block fabrics, cut out pieces according to individual block directions.

FROM WHITE SOLID FABRIC, CUT THE FOLLOWING LENGTHWISE:

- ❏ 2 strips 6" × 60½ " (15 × 154.5 cm).

- ❏ 2 strips 8" × 59½" (20.5 × 151 cm).

FROM SAMPLER BLOCK SCRAPS, CUT:

- ❏ Strips 2½" (6.5 cm) wide × varying lengths from 4" to 18" (10 to 45.5 cm).

Blocks

UNFINISHED BLOCK: 12½" × 12½" (31.5 × 31.5 cm)

Follow the individual block instructions to make one each of twenty sampler blocks.

Quilt Top

1 Refer to the quilt photo to lay out the quilt top in five rows of four blocks each. Sew the rows together, and press seams for each row in alternating directions. Sew the rows together. Press.

2 To add the borders, sew a white strip 6" × 60½" (15 × 154.5 cm) to each long side of the pieced top. Trim the ends of the border strips so they are even with the pieced blocks.

3 Sew the white strips 8" × 59½" (20.5 × 151 cm) to the top and bottom edges of the quilt. Trim the ends of the strips so the corners of the quilt top are square.

4 Make a quilt sandwich with the backing, batting, and quilt top. Baste the layers and quilt as desired. This quilt has a beautiful and varied combination of quilting patterns, including flowers, echo quilting, and straight lines. Trim the batting and backing to match the quilt top.

6 Join the binding strips end to end to make a continuous 275" (6.98 m) length. Bind the raw edges to finish the quilt.

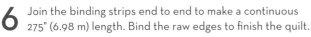

SAMPLER QUILT IN SOLIDS

Designed and made by Katie Clark Blakesley

FINISHED SIZE: 63" × 80" (160 × 203.2 cm)

TECHNIQUES USED: Foundation piecing, partial seams

SKILL LEVEL: Intermediate

DESIGN NOTE: Adding Block Borders and Sashing

This quilt uses a traditional grid pattern with sashing. It omits the outside border and swaps traditional white sashing for a warm, neutral-colored solid. Narrow solid borders around each block, as well as cornerstones, provide additional, unexpected elements. Using all solid fabrics in the blocks as well as the other elements gives this quilt a crisp, clean look.

What should you do when your piecing is not perfect? The narrow block borders fill a functional as well as graphic role. Adding small borders on the sampler quilt is an excellent way to hide small mistakes. If you find that a few of your sampler blocks are just under 12½" × 12½" (31.5 × 31.5 cm), adding borders and then trimming all of the blocks to 14" × 14" (35.5 × 35.5 cm) will give you a little bit of wiggle room without altering the look of the quilt. Embrace the beauty, uniqueness, and even slight imperfections of handmade.

Make the Sampler Quilt in Solids

Fabric amounts and instructions for all twenty classic blocks can be found throughout this book. Refer to the visual block index on page 9 for specific page locations.

Materials

All fabric amounts are for 45" (114.5 cm) wide fabric.

- Fabric as needed for the selected twenty sampler blocks
- 1⅓ yd (122 cm) of neutral-colored solid sashing fabric
- 6 fat quarters *total* (18" × 22") (45.5 × 56 cm) of different solid-color framing fabrics
- ½ yd (45.5 cm) additional solid-color framing fabric
- 4⅔ yd (4.2 m) backing fabric
- 71" × 88" (180.3 × 223.5 cm) low-loft cotton batting
- ¾ yd (68.5 cm) binding fabric

Tools

- Template patterns for foundation-pieced blocks
- Foundation-piecing paper
- Hera marker or water-soluble pen

Cutting

From sampler block fabrics, cut out pieces according to individual block directions.

FROM NEUTRAL SOLID-COLOR SASHING FABRIC, CUT:

❑ 31 strips 3½" × 14" (9 × 35.5 cm).

FROM SOLID-COLOR FRAMING FABRICS, CUT:

❑ 12 squares 3½" × 3½" (9 x9 cm).*

FROM ½ YD SOLID-COLOR FRAMING FABRIC, CUT:

❑ 8 strips 1¾" × 12½" (4.5 × 31.5 cm) and 8 strips 1¾" × 15" (4.5 × 38 cm).

FROM EACH OF FOUR SOLID-COLOR FRAMING FABRICS, CUT:

❑ 6 strips 1¾" × 12½" (4.5 × 31.5 cm) and 6 strips 1¾" × 15" (4.5 × 38 cm).

FROM EACH OF TWO SOLID-COLOR FRAMING FABRICS, CUT:

❑ 4 strips 1¾" × 12½" (4.5 × 31.5 cm) and 4 strips 1¾" × 15" (4.5 × 38 cm).

FROM BINDING FABRIC, CUT:

❑ 8 strips 2½" (6.5 cm) × width of fabric.

Cut at least one square from each fabric.

Bordered blocks

UNFINISHED BLOCK: 14" × 14" (35.5 × 35.5 cm)

1 Follow the individual block instructions to make one each of twenty sampler blocks, each measuring 12½" × 12½" (31.5 × 31.5 cm) unfinished.

2 Arrange the blocks in a grid, four blocks across and five blocks down as shown in the Sampler in Solids Construction Diagram, or to your own liking.

Tip
I recommend placing the block wrong side up when sewing on the borders. With the back seams exposed, it is easier to see seam intersections, and you are less likely to cut off points.

3 To frame the blocks, sew a colored strip 1¾" × 12½" (4.5 × 31.5 cm) to the top and bottom edge of the block. Press.

4 Sew the matching strips 1¾" × 15" (4.5 × 38 cm) to the block sides. Press. Backstitch at the beginning and end of each seam when you sew on the borders.

5 Repeat Steps 3 and 4 to add borders to all twenty blocks.

6 Trim each block to 14" × 14" (35.5 × 35.5 cm). Take care to trim evenly around each block—there should be about 1" (2.5 cm) of the solid border on each side after trimming.

Quilt Top

1 Lay out the bordered blocks in the same grid again, four across and five down. Place the thirty-one vertical and horizontal sashing strips 3½" × 14" (9 × 35.5 cm) and the twelve cornerstones 3½" × 3½" (9 × 9 cm) between the blocks.

Note: Blocks may be rotated from their original orientation to give a slightly different look to this quilt.

2 Sew the first row of blocks together, adding sashing strips between blocks. Repeat for the additional four rows of blocks. Press all seams toward the sashing.

3 To make the four rows of sashing/cornerstones—sew together the horizontal sashing pieces and cornerstones end to end. Press all seams toward the sashing.

4 Sew the first row of sashing to the first row of blocks, aligning seams. Backstitch at the beginning and the end. Repeat with each of the remaining four rows of blocks and three rows of sashing. Press and trim the quilt top if necessary.

5 Make a quilt sandwich with the backing, batting, and quilt top. Baste the layers and quilt as desired. I used an allover meandering pattern in the borders and quilted different free-motion designs in each of the blocks. Trim the batting and backing to match the quilt top.

6 Join the binding strips to make a continuous length. Bind the raw edges to finish the quilt.

Sampler in Solids Construction Diagram

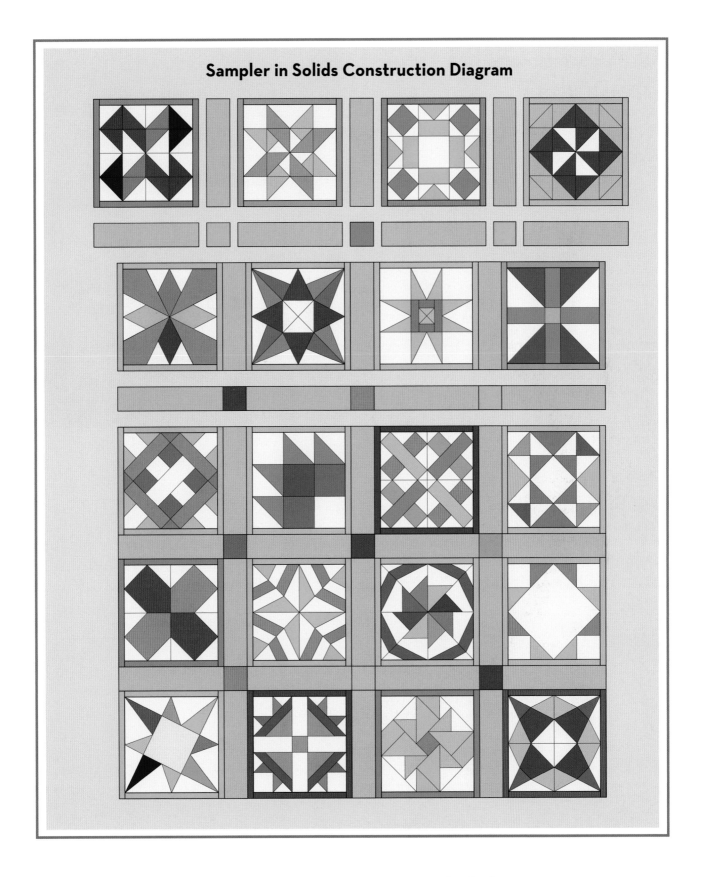

SAMPLER QUILT ON-POINT

Designed and made by **Faith Jones**

FINISHED SIZE: 72" × 90" (182.9 × 228.6 cm)

TECHNIQUES USED: Foundation piecing, partial seams

SKILL LEVEL: Intermediate

DESIGN NOTE: Enlarging a Quilt

When I design and create a quilt, I almost always lean toward something lap size. Perhaps it's just my comfort zone, perhaps it's because that size is easiest to quilt on my home machine. But there are occasions where I want to make something a bit larger. Bed-sized quilts can be made with intricately pieced blocks from top to bottom. Sometimes though, it's nice to enlarge your quilt—and showcase your blocks more effectively—by adding simple repeating blocks between the sampler blocks. A "pop" of color in the center of each block adds interest. I used squares, but consider piecing in small Sawtooth Stars or an equally simple but effective pattern. Common elements repeating throughout the quilt have the ability to pull the overall quilt design together and create a cohesive piece.

Make the Sampler On-Point Quilt

Fabric amounts and instructions for all twenty classic blocks can be found throughout this book. Refer to the visual block index on page 9 for specific page locations.

Materials

All fabric amounts are for 45" (114.5 cm) wide fabric.

- Fabric as needed for the selected twenty sampler blocks
- 4 yd white solid fabric (repeating blocks)
- 1 yd (91.5 cm) *total* of a variety of print and/or solid fabrics (block center)
- 5½ yd (5.03 m) backing fabric
- 80" × 98" (203.2 × 248.9 cm) low-loft cotton batting
- ⅔ yd (61 cm) binding fabric

Tools

- Template patterns for foundation-pieced blocks
- Foundation-piecing paper
- Hera marker or water-soluble pen

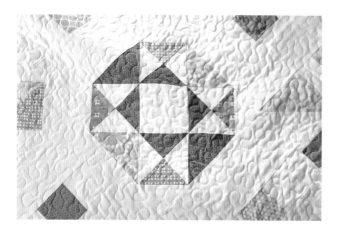

Cutting

From sampler block fabrics, cut out pieces according to individual block directions.

FROM WHITE SOLID FABRIC, CUT:

❒ 60 rectangles 3½" × 5¼" (9 × 13.15 cm).

❒ 60 strips 5¼" × 13" (13.5 × 33 cm).

FROM PRINT AND SOLID FABRICS, CUT:

❒ 30 squares 3½" × 3½" (9 × 9 cm).

FROM BINDING FABRIC, CUT:

❒ 9 strips 2½" (6.5 cm) × width of fabric.

Blocks

UNFINISHED BLOCK: 12½" × 12½" (31.5 × 31.5 cm)

Make twenty sampler blocks and thirty simple repeating blocks.

1 Follow the individual block instructions to make one each of twenty sampler blocks, each measuring 12½" × 12½" (31.5 × 31.5 cm) unfinished. Set aside.

2 To make the simple repeating blocks, sew a white rectangle 3½" × 5¼" (9 × 13.5 cm) to each side of a colored square 3½" × 3½" (9 × 9 cm) to make the middle block row *(fig. 1)*. Press.

3 Sew a white strip 5¼" × 13" (13.5 × 33 cm) to the top and bottom. Press and trim the resulting 13" × 13" (33 × 33 cm) block to 12½" × 12½" (31.5 × 31.5 cm). Repeat to make a total of thirty blocks.

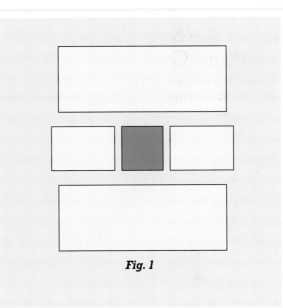

Fig. 1

Quilt Top

1 Lay out all fifty blocks on-point as shown *(fig. 2)*.

Note: Blocks may be rotated from their original orientation to give a slightly different look to this quilt.

2 The white blocks along the edges—three at the top, three at the bottom, and four on each side—will need to be trimmed. Cut each block diagonally *(fig. 3)*, allowing for ¼" (6 mm) seam allowance along the trimmed edge.

3 Trim the four corner blocks. Cut each block diagonally *(fig. 4)*, allowing for ¼" (6 mm) seam allowance along each cut edge.

4 Refer to the Sampler On-Point Construction Diagram to sew the blocks together, on-point, into eight diagonal rows. Press.

5 Sew together the diagonal rows and the corner pieces to create a finished quilt top. Press the seams open to reduce bulk.

6 Make a quilt sandwich with the backing, batting, and quilt top. Baste the layers and quilt as desired. I used an allover meandering design. Trim the batting and backing to match the quilt top.

7 Join the binding strips to make a continuous length. Bind the raw edges to finish the quilt.

Fig. 2

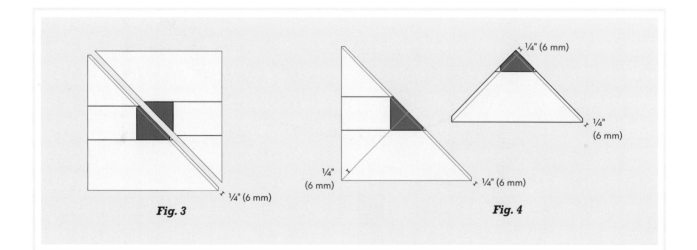

Fig. 3

Fig. 4

¼" (6 mm)

¼" (6 mm)

¼" (6 mm)

¼" (6 mm)

¼" (6 mm)

Sampler On-Point Construction Diagram

Template Patterns

The CD included with this book contains these template patterns, all at full size. Instructions for downloading and printing the patterns are on the CD.

Stardust Quilt

- Riviera Template A
- Riviera Template B
- Dakota Star Foundation Piecing Template
- Dakota Star Cutting Template

Dancing Squares Baby Quilt

- Rolling Squares Template
- Flying Geese Template (optional)

Cross Point Quilt

- Red Cross Template A
- Red Cross Template B

New World Pouch

- Mayflower Block Template
- Mini Mayflower Pouch Template

Crosspatch Bag

- Crosspatch Block Template A
- Crosspatch Block Template B
- Crosspatch Bag Block Template A
- Crosspatch Bag Block Template B

Spin It Again Quilt

- Wheel of Fortune Template A
- Wheel of Fortune Template B

Cosmos Baby Quilt

- Tilted Star Template

Seaside Quilt

- Cross and Crown Template

Star Bright Quilt

- Exploding Star Template A
- Exploding Star Template B

Cut Glass Baby Quilt

- Geometric Star Template A
- Geometric Star Template B
- Geometric Star Template C

Double Dutch Table Runner

- Double Windmill Template A
- Double Windmill Template B

Rainbow Mosaic Pillow

- Rainbow Mosaic Template A
- Rainbow Mosaic Template B
- Rainbow Mosaic Template C
- Rainbow Mosaic Template D

Bibliography

Beyer, Jinny. *The Quilters Album of Patchwork Patterns*. Elmhurst, Illinois: Breckling Press, 2009.

Brackman, Barbara. *Encyclopedia of Pieced Quilt Patterns*. Paducah, Kentucky: American Quilter's Society, 1993.

———. *Making History: Quilts and Fabric from 1890-1970*. Lafayette, California: C & T Publishing, 2008.

———. *Patterns of History, 1930-1950: Pick a Pack—Pick a Pattern*. Kansas City: Kansas City Star Books, 2004.

———. *Women of Design: Quilts in the Newspaper*. Kansas City: Kansas City Star Books, 2004.

Shaw, Robert. *American Quilts: The Democratic Art, 1780-2007*. New York: Sterling Publishing, 2009.

Websites
Modern Quilt Guild

themodernquiltguild.com

International Quilt Study Center and Museum

quiltstudy.org

Quilt History

womenfolk.com

theamishquilt.com

quilthistory.com

ladiesartcompany.com/history

folkartmuseum.org

barbarabrackman.blogspot.com

quilterbydesign.com/lessons/paper_piecing_history

roberteshaw.com

About the Authors

Katie Clark Blakesley   www.swimbikequilt.com

Katie is an avid quilter who also enjoys triathlon. She is happy to have found a way to combine quilting and her academic interest in American women's history and material culture. Katie is past president of the Washington, D.C., Modern Quilt Guild. Each summer, she organizes "100 Quilts for Kids," for which quilters can sew and donate quilts to kids in their own community. Katie's work has been featured in *Sweet Celebrations with Moda Bake Shop Chefs* (Stash Books), *Quiltmaker's 100 Blocks, Fat Quarterly e-zine, Quilt It Today, Quilty,* and the *Moda Bake Shop.* She teaches classes at local quilt shops and enjoys giving lectures and presentations to modern and traditional guilds. Katie lives in Alexandria, Virginia, with her husband and two children.

Lee Heinrich   www.freshlypieced.com

As a graphic designer, Lee spent more than ten years designing publications and other printed materials. She began sewing and quilting in 2008 and sees modern quilting as a natural extension of her design work. Lee's quilts and other sewing projects have been featured in *Modern Quilts From the Blogging Universe* (Martingale), *Quiltmaker* magazine, *Fons & Porter's Easy Quilts* magazine, *Sew Mama Sew, Fat Quarterly e-zine,* the *Moda Bake Shop,* and others. Lee's "Lifesavers" quilt took first place in the Modern Traditionalism, Small Quilts category at QuiltCon, a national modern quilt show, in 2013. Lee also sells patterns, teaches at quilt shops and retreats, and gives presentations to guilds about modern quilting and the online quilting community. Lee is a member of the Milwaukee Modern Quilt Guild. She lives in Milwaukee, Wisconsin, with her husband and two daughters.

Faith Jones   www.freshlemonsquilts.com

Faith began sewing at a young age and started quilting in early 2009. As she delved into modern quilting, Faith became intrigued by the process of using historically traditional blocks in modern, nontraditional ways. In addition to blogging—developing tutorials, hosting quilt-alongs, and creating and sharing patterns—Faith speaks at modern and traditional quilt guilds and teaches at quilting/sewing retreats. Faith's patterns can be found in several publications: *Modern Blocks: 99 Blocks from Your Favorite Designers, Fat Quarterly e-zine, Quiltmaker* magazine, and *100 Blocks* issues, *Fons & Porter Scrap Quilts, Quilty, Modern Quilts Unlimited,* and *Modern Quilting Magazine* (U.K.). Faith lives in the Chicago, Illinois, suburbs with her husband and two children.

Index

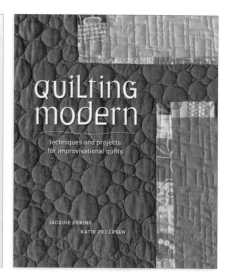